Nannie

A memoir by Jane Bloom

www.yourmemoir.co.uk

This book was written with the assistance of Your Memoir. For further information contact Marnie Summerfield Smith via yourmemoir.co.uk marnie@yourmemoir.co.uk or by calling 07710 721389.

ISBN 978-1-78972-348-9

Be content with what you've got. Always wanting what you've not.
Ada Nicholls

Contents

Acknowledgements

Thanks to the Leiston Writing Group that started in 1987 and is still going strong, in particular to Michael Laskey who has always encouraged me to keep going with my writing and not to give up.

Thank you to Marnie Summerfield Smith for her advice, her belief in what I have written and for guiding me through the process.

Thanks to my husband Gary for his support and encouragement.

Most of all to my grandmother for the stability and wisdom she gave me that I did not appreciate at the time.

With love to my Mum, Mary,
who once told me I would write a book.

Introduction

I lived with my grandmother from the age of four until I was 19. I felt her presence and feel her influence still. Over the years I have written much about my grandmother, so much so, that I thought I had nothing more to add. That was until a friend read what I had written and asked me some questions. She wanted to know what I would like to have asked my grandmother. I thought about it and realized that I would like to have known what her childhood was like, what clothes she wore, what sort of schooling she had and what her brothers and sisters were like. I would want to know about her home and where in Northampton it was, the food she ate and the games she played. I would want stories about her parents and her grandparents and any ancestors she could remember. I have a picture of her grandfather, William Crane, who was born in the early 1820s. It would have been interesting to know more about him.

A friend commented that there was very little dialogue between my grandmother and myself in my writings. I recall learning that my grandmother used to have to sit with her forearms against her waist and her elbows pushed back so a wooden yardstick could be slipped between the gaps in front of her elbows when she sat at the table. It was a way to make her sit up straight when she ate her meal. I still have my grandmother's yardstick, so-called because it is three-feet long and three feet make a yard. I have used it for measuring when making curtains. I cannot hear my grandmother's voice telling me about the stick. I don't remember having a conversation with her. I remember myself as a silent child who watched from the shadows, learning from an early age just to observe.

Recently I went to visit my two youngest great grandchildren who live in Rendlesham. They are the children of my granddaughter Laura and her husband, Shane Marks. Jasper is a rumbustious little boy who had just turned two and loves his food. His sister, five-year-old Lydia, is a more delicate looking child, slender, dark haired and full of fun. As I watched Lydia, my mind drifted to thoughts about my grandmother's sister, Great Aunt Alice. I remember her as an old lady with ill health and wispy grey hair. I became mesmerised watching Laura's children and tried to imagine Alice as a young, bright eyed, happy child full of curiosity playing with her sister Ada, my grandmother.

I regret not asking my grandmother more about her life and her parents and grandparents and what her life was like as a child. I wish I had asked my mother more questions about her time as a child. I hope what I have written will be of interest to my grandchildren, great grandchildren and all the future generations.

Chapter One

Twenty or so years ago, I was given a copy of the family tree that Richard Mann, a distant cousin, had researched. The oldest ancestor went back to John Eyles ca 1760. There was no mention of whom he had married.

John had five children, one of whom was George whose daughter Elizabeth married William Crane. They had four children and it was their son Thomas who married my great grandmother, Emma Charlotte Smith. They had seven children: William, Kate, my grandmother Ada born in 1882, Herbert, Alice, Frederick and Harry. Alice and Kate lived together in Northampton. When Auntie Alice was 17 she had all her teeth out. She told me one of the saddest things that I have ever heard. "I cried and cried after having my teeth out," she said, "because I thought no-one would ever want to marry me, and no-one ever did."

In 1907, my grandmother Ada married Tom Nicholls. He was from the Aylesham area of Norfolk. They married at St Sepulcher's Church, Northampton on May 20, 1907. The invitation was sent from 17, South Cottage, Framlingham where my grandmother was living with her aunt Emma Crane.

Tom's surname had originally been Nickolds and was changed in the mid-1880s by Tom's grandfather. Tom worked for EG Clarke, who were a seed and corn merchant. When he married Ada, they continued living with Aunt Emma at 17, Albert Road. They had three children. William (Bill), born on May 27, 1908 and Gladys Winnifred Marjorie, born on February 23, 1913. I couldn't say Gladys when I was a toddler, only Dah, and the nickname stuck. I never called her aunt. She went out to work, something to do with insurance I think, collecting premiums maybe. She hadn't a car so used a bike.

My mother Mary was born on April 24, 1911. She married Arthur Webber at Framlingham Church on the April 13, 1942. Arthur came from Chard in Somerset. He was in the army and they met when he was stationed in Framlingham. I was born in 1944 and was their only child. Their divorce became absolute on November 16, 1950.

***

The faces in the picture stare back at me. I had seen a copy of this picture at Framlingham Castle. It was an exhibition of local people who had gone off to fight in the First World War. The year was 2012 and at the time I had seven grandchildren and two great grandchildren.

Thoughts of my ancestors stayed with me. One day, as I handed around the ham sandwiches to my visiting grandchildren, I thought about how I was their ancestor – someone they might talk about in their old age. "Do you remember Nan and all her cooking?" they might say.

My grandfather was killed in the First World War. The impact of those words hit me as I write them down. His name is on a memorial in the churchyard: TW Nicholls, Lance

Corporal. Household Battalion. As a child I would walk through the churchyard, glancing at the stone memorial with daisies growing around it. A list of names, that was all it was.

"That's your grandfather's name there," my mother would say to me. "Thomas William Nicholls." As I grew up, I learned that my grandmother did not know where my grandfather had been killed or what battle it was. She only knew it was in France. As I got older my mother spoke of her father, but I was caught up with the present rather than the past so did not pay attention.

"I was only six when he died," my mother told me, "but I can remember him so well. Especially the last time I saw him." She would then sigh and hug me, and I would wriggle free to get away from the sadness. She talked about him, telling me how he used to take his children down to the seaside at Thorpeness, 12 miles away. He would hire a small pony and trap and they would all go off for the day. I felt that my mother, the baby of the family, had been his favourite. I never heard my grandmother mention her husband's name.

In later years I found a faded black and white picture of my grandfather in his uniform. He had a small moustache and looked serious. Years later when going through old photos, I found one which had been sent as a postcard to my grandmother with her name and address on. The words written on the back were, "For you dark eyes, with love from Tom." Those words brought him to life for me.

A talk had been given by the local historical society about Framlingham during the First World War. I went to see if I could piece the puzzle together, but instead I learned about poverty and how very young people had to work to

take the place of the people who went to fight in the Great
War and how the men were persuaded to go off and fight.
I gleaned that the Household Battalion no longer existed
because everyone in the battalion had been killed. I gained
no information about the man Thomas William Nicholls.
Walking home in the dark afterwards, I thought of the terrible
waste and sadness to the family of Thomas Nicholls who had
gone off to war to fight for his country and had not returned.

Thomas William Nicholls, born in 1878, was killed in the
Great War on May 3, 1917 at the Battle of the Scarpe in Rouex
near Arras, France. At first my grandmother was told he had
been captured, it was not until April 1918 that she received the
telegram to say that he had been killed. She thought he had lost
his memory and was somewhere alive in France. She looked out
for the postman each day, hoping for better news, walking to
the end of Albert Road to meet him. I absorbed this habit from
my grandmother. I have always looked out for the postman and
I still do. The road she lived on was nicknamed Widows' Road
due to how many women whose husbands had died in the war
were living there. It was like that in 1914.

I know little of how my grandmother managed financially
to bring up my mother and her two other children, Gladys
and Bill. She was an expert needlewoman, so maybe that was
a way for her to make money. Her brother Bert was a dentist
in Northampton and her sisters Kitty and Alice were both
schoolteachers. Maybe they helped.

Aside from the practicalities, I don't know how my
grandmother coped emotionally with the death of her
husband. I know that she was a very proud woman. She once
went to get free coal, which widows from the parish were

entitled to. I remember my mother telling me that when my grandmother came home she said, "Never again will I ask for charity and be humiliated in the way I was."

Nannie used to say, "Smile and the world smiles with you. Cry and you cry alone." She said a lot of things, my Nannie. I never saw her cry, but she did seem to smile quite a bit. I do remember that. I don't remember her hugging me, but I can't remember many hugs anyway. My Mum was very much loved by her father. When he died, this love and security vanished, and my mother was cast adrift. She was bought up partly in the Edwardian era, so was ill equipped to cope with happenings in her later life. She was 31 when she married my father. I was told that he was a charming, well-spoken man who reminded my mother of her own father, maybe because of his army uniform. My mother had no way of knowing that he was an alcoholic or that he could be violent when drunk. Their marriage lasted six years during which time they lived in Taunton. My mother's neighbours, Alf and Marjorie Ridgeway, were concerned for my mother's welfare and contacted my grandmother. She hired a car and had a friend drive her to Somerset to collect my mother and I. My mother divorced my father for mental cruelty. The divorce scarred her since divorce was considered to be shameful at that time. My mother was even refused communion at the local church because she was a divorced woman. Her physical health deteriorated as she got older and after a stomach operation in her mid-40s she suffered a breakdown. She never understood why she had got depressed or how to cope with the misery of it. She never recovered her joie de vivre after that. She did remarry at the age of 60, but unknown to her, her second husband had a troubled past. She was naïve. I don't think that she was able to cope with men and marriage. A further depression followed when her husband John, my stepfather, took his own life in 1972.

My mother continued living at 13, Albert Road until she died in 1984. She had been born at number 17, moving down to number 13 when she was two. I was born at number 13. I left in 1963 to get married, returning to number 14 in 1974. These houses are not next door to each other. It was a quirk of building back then. As my mother lived on the same road as me, I saw her most days. An elderly aunt of my stepfather had left number 14 to him when she died, but he never lived there. Nowadays when I walk up and down Albert Road, I have the memory of six generations on this road: my grandmother, my mother, my children, my grandchildren, my great grandchildren and myself.

My mother never had the strength of character for coping that her mother had, but people remarked on how kind she was. She always wanted to make life right for others, in a way that she could not make life right for herself. Her greatest pleasure were my three children, her grandchildren. They have good memories of the lady who always had sweets in her pocket, a smile on her face and a hug to give them.

My mother died in hospital of bladder and bone cancer. I remember her saying to me, "My mother wouldn't let me suffer like this." I took it to mean that her mother would have looked after her as no one else did. She had, after all, rescued her from an abusive marriage.

Did the death of her father at a young age affect her for the rest of her life? I think it did. I too grew up without a father and I am an only child. People ask if I mind that. The only child bit is fine, as I quite like the independence of being an only one. Being used to my own company stood me in good stead when my husband John died. I have, however, always minded not having a father who cared about me. Even now I think what a difference it could have made to my life. When I was 24, I went down to Devon with my husband and two children to find my father. I found out which pub he was in and asked someone if they would mind asking him to come outside. He had heard I was in Chard and stumbled out of the pub saying, "I expect your mother is a rich lady now. Have you got any money?" I gave him five pounds and a Daily Mirror. I invited him to a meal at my uncle's, his brother, the next day. He did come, eating a small amount of the roast turkey that I cooked for him and wrapping some of it in a napkin to take home with him – explaining that he wasn't used to eating large meals. After my first husband's death, my son said to me, "It isn't like divorce is it Mum, at least I knew my Dad loved me."

Growing up, my father became just a name. The only good thing I heard about him was when I passed my driving test. "You are like your father," my mother told me. "He was a good driver."

I see families together and wonder what if would have been like to be part of a complete family. I do feel I have missed out and that the death of my grandfather caused ripples that ran through the family and changed the destiny of what might have been.

***

Like the poppy seeds in the Flanders fields from long ago, the events of the Great War and the Second World War cast seeds into my family that took hold and grew, affecting members of my family and their descendants. The sadness and anxiety that were there when I was a child lingered and although both wars are now long over, the sorrow remains with those who lived with the grieving. It gave the house I grew up in a sad atmosphere, untouched by light.

I know nothing of my grandfather's childhood. He had a sister called Beatrice, spoken of as Auntie Trixie. When I was 16, my grandmother, mother and myself went to Ebbw Vale in Wales to see her. I had short hair and my waist was narrow then. I wore a green skirt, a white jumper and a pair of flat, white shoes. Ebbw Vale was full of small houses with tiny front gardens into which sheep wandered. Aunt Trixie was short and round with her hair wound into a bun on top of her head. I hadn't realised she was my grandfather's sister and even if I had known, I don't suppose I would have asked any questions about him. Now I would love to have known what he was like as a boy, a child, a teenager.

My mother's brother Bill died in the Second World War a year before I was born. My grandmother had been immensely proud of Bill. He had gone to the local public school on a scholarship. He had been offered a place as head boy if he had become a boarder, but he remained as a dayboy. A local historian told me he was a brilliant student who had won every available award. He then went onto Emmanuel College, Cambridge. After graduation, he taught in Hull where he met and married his wife Betty. They had their first daughter, Pip in 1940 and their second daughter, Anne, was due to be born in June, 1943. Sadly, Bill died in March of that year, three months before his wife gave birth. One year later his sister, my mother, gave birth to me, so Bill was always in the past to me.

I expect she would have liked a boy because of her brother. She said that if I had been a boy I would have been called Michael.

I was told Bill thought the world of his two sisters and mother. My mother had to cope with the deaths of two men she had loved.

Dead people became like ghosts, shadows of people who cast long shadows into the future. My mother carried the sadness and grief all her life. When I hear on the news that another soldier has been killed and another child or children have been left fatherless, I turn away not wanting to see their sad faces, knowing that a family has been deprived of knowing their father and that they too will grow up with the long shadows of the dead.

Chapter Two

Ada Nicholls nee Crane was one of seven children. I believe that her father, whose name was Tom – the same as her husband – was a jeweller and goldsmith in Gold Street, Northampton, which is where the family lived, but I can't be sure. I know nothing about her early life and I have no pictures of her as a child. I never heard my grandmother talk about what it was like when she was a child, where she lived, or about her brothers and sisters. The only thing I learned was that she had lived in Northampton and that she came to Framlington in Suffolk to help her aunt, Emma Crane, in a milliner's shop.

I was given my grandmother's name as my second name. She hated the name Ada, as did I. I am told she used to give her name as May. I rubbed the Ada off my birth certificate, although I have now put it back. It isn't on any of my official documents and whenever I am asked for my name I say: "Just plain Jane." None of my family or friends knows what it is, despite trying to guess. I think now I should be proud that I was given my grandmother's name.

When I was four years old, my mother and I returned to Framlingham to live with my 67-year-old grandmother. I have vivid memories of the house we lived in. It stood at the end of a row of semi-detached Victorian houses, on a dusty unmade road. Albert Villas was the name on a cream plaque in the centre of the brickwork. The number on the door was 13, but I am not superstitious. The house had a bay window and a solid wooden front door with a black, cast-iron knocker. Winter jasmine grew around the door, flowering in a yellow mass in the bleak months of December and January. In the small flowerbed at the front of the house there were polyanthus, stocks and Michaelmas daisies.

There were no streetlights near the house. As a child, on dark evenings, I approached the house with my heart pounding, always thinking that there was someone around the corner waiting to jump out at me.

Inside the house everything was brown. The front room carpet was a dark brown, worn at the edges where the carpet moths had laid eggs. Bill had bought his mother this carpet with his first earnings as teacher. The front room had a large bay window. In the summer time a shiny copper tray stood on a wooden stand on top of which was a bowl with a maiden-hair fern in. The wallpaper was orange with brown squares on. A brown wool curtain covered the door. Around the fireplace were dark blue, shiny glazed tiles. On the mantelshelf were ornaments and a photograph of Bill on his wedding day.

In the corner stood a piano. Who played it? Not anyone that I could remember. Maybe it was just traditional to have a piano. As a child I had fingered the keys and from the book propped up against the lid I had learnt to play nursery rhymes; Baa Baa Black Sheep, Hot Cross Buns and Lavenders' Blue, with one finger. The long passage to this room intimidated me. The light bulb in the hall hung from a long brown flex and when the light was switched on a dim light showed through the orange light shade. In the winter time this cast shadows, which frightened me when I walked down the hallway. The room seemed separate from the other rooms and was only used at Christmas, on special Sundays and in the summer to play when my cousins, Pip and Anne, came to stay with their mother, Bill's widow, my Auntie Betty. The house came to life then, the atmosphere changed and even the front room seemed different.

The view from the front room window was out onto the dusty road. I would look out, waiting, hopeful, fearful, never knowing why I was frightened or what I was waiting for. My mother had been frightened of my father. Years later I was told this was because he'd said he would hurt me to get at her. I suppose her fear transported itself to me. When I looked out of the front room window, I noticed the unevenness of the glass, which distorted the view. It seemed better to be out of doors. Inside, looking out, a sense of bleakness would envelope me.

As I grew older, returning from school, I would enter the house from the back, peering around the corner at the top of the yard not wanting to be seen. I would look into the dining room window and see my aunt and grandmother winding thin strips of coloured material, called bias binding, onto narrow cards, before labelling them and wrapping them into cellophane. They would then count them into dozens and secure each bundle with an elastic band, ready to return to the local factory. My heart would sink and I would try to get indoors before my always irritable aunt saw me. I never managed to do this though and once indoors my aunt would say, "Shush, Mrs. Dale's Diary is on," and the radio would be turned up. I would feel as if I was an intrusion, a nuisance. I would get a drink and a biscuit and go to my room. My mother wasn't there during the day as she worked in a local office as a secretary. She made it clear that she didn't enjoy going out to work. She told me that she'd sold her wedding ring to buy me a pair of shoes. I didn't like my mum not being at home when I got in from school.

Near the kitchen was a pantry, with a flaking whitewashed ceiling and walls. A wooden food safe was kept in there. It had thick metal gauze on the door to keep the flies out. My grandmother kept her provisions on a high shelf in her pantry. Also in there were homemade jams and marmalade, onions she had pickled, tinned fruit, pears, pineapple and peaches, with tins of evaporated milk for Sunday lunch; plus cartons of custard powder, boxes of Burdall's gravy salt and a tub of Cadbury's drinking chocolate. How I loved that!

On the floor was a galvanized tin bucket with a lid that would be filled with Isinglass in which eggs were preserved. The eggs would be placed in the liquid, which would set around them. They could only be used for baking.

One morning I went to the pantry to fetch the milk jug that stood on a shelf. I poured the milk onto my cereal and two grey mice floated out of the jug. There were always mice traps in the house, but these two had met a different death.

Upstairs at the end of the landing was the small narrow bedroom where I slept. This room overlooked the town and from the window I could see the different coloured rooftops of the houses and beyond them the sky. In the late summer I would see the swallows lined up on the telegraph wires preparing for their flight back to Africa. There was just enough space in this room for a narrow bed and a bookcase behind the head of it. At night as I fell asleep I would see a long shadow on

the wall. I thought it was a figure of a man and I would bury
my head under the bedclothes, but years later I discovered it
was the shadow from the door made by the hall light falling
against it. My mother would say goodnight to me. I would
listen to her footsteps getting fainter and fainter as she went
downstairs. I would feel so alone and far away from everyone.

I suppose I felt loved, but I never felt safe or secure. I
learned to bury my feelings. I was never asked what I wanted.
Despite all this I have grown up into a very practical person,
like my grandmother, capable and competent, very good in an
emergency. I love babies and children. I am told that I am not
good at having fun and being light hearted, but that I am a
fantastic organiser.

Next to my room was my grandmother's bedroom, which
was the room where I'd been born. Her bedroom was at the
front of the house upstairs and she slept on a double bed
with a metal frame and a feather mattress, which I remember
pummeling to make the feathers soft again after a night's
sleep. Also in that bedroom was a fireplace – a fire was never
lit in my time – a mantelshelf with a picture of her son's
wedding featuring my mother as a bridesmaid. Then there
was a pine washstand on which stood a washbowl and a jug.
I still have the bowl and use it to hold cut up Seville oranges
when I make marmalade in January. At Christmas I put fruit
in it with brandy to steep for the Christmas cake. Also on the
washstand were a hairbrush and an assortment of hairgrips,
which my grandmother used to pin her grey hair into a roll
at the back of her neck, and a soap dish with flannels on.
That dish and the smell of the wet flannels are my strongest
memory. It is a smell that I still associate with old people.

In a corner of the room was a large wardrobe in which were my grandmother's clothes, including a moth-eaten fur coat. There were cotton day dresses, winter skirts and a grey suit. At the bottom of the wardrobe were piles of thick stockings, shoes and corsets. My grandmother always wore a body-length corset stiffened with whale bones and fastened with a long row of hooks. This was worn over her vest, next would go on a pink petticoat made from a shiny knitted type material called stockinet.

We didn't have an indoor lavatory, just a chamber pot under the bed in each of the four bedrooms. Every morning Nannie, did what was called "the slops", which meant emptying all the chamber pots. For this she had a white enamel bucket with a lid. After the slops, she would dust through the house. The house was her domain, although it was rented, but many were in those days. The owner was a man called Prinny Cooper who kept a boot and shoe shop in Castle Street, Framlingham the town where we lived.

Upstairs at the back of the house was the large bedroom where my mother slept. In here was a fireplace and two beds. I would sleep in this room with my mother when I was ill. A fire would be lit and the sheets changed each time the doctor came. The sheets felt crisp and clean and the room would become warm and feel cosy with the light and warmth from the fire. It made being ill rather glorious. It was lovely being snuggled down in bed in a warm room watching the flames flicker making firelight patterns on the ceiling, especially as dusk came. There wasn't a hearth upstairs and as the coals would fall onto the few tiles that had been laid in front of it, a fireguard would be put in front of the lit fire. Lighting the fire was the same procedure as in other rooms, except my grandmother had to struggle up the stairs with the sticks, coal and ash pan.

My childhood illnesses included whooping cough, measles, blood poisoning, mumps, dysentery and chicken pox to name a few. I spent a fair amount of time in bed. Back in the 1950s any illness, even chicken pox, could keep children in bed for weeks. My mother's fussing was understandable. Penicillin had only become available for general use in 1945. Before then, childhood illnesses were often fatal. When I was ill I would have, at the very least, a week in bed with the doctor calling daily. Once on the mend I would be allowed to get up in the afternoon for an hour or two and then longer, and then a week after that I could go out for a short walk. I always felt weak. Looking back, I realise that the weakness I felt after being ill was a consequence of all that lying about and being treated like an invalid. In the early 70s I was childminding my GP's 18-month-old daughter. It was a warm summer's evening and his daughter was running around outside in just a cotton vest even though she had chicken pox. I was horrified, but I was told, "We don't keep children in bed nowadays, unless there is really something the matter. Chicken pox is nothing."

When I was unwell, my mother would read me stories. Although I could read by the age of four, like most children I loved being read to. My favourite were the Enid Blyton books such as The Faraway Tree, The Wishing Chair, Cherry Tree Farm, Secret Seven and Famous Five series. I loved Mr. Galliano's Circus and The Castle of Adventure. I had the weekly Sunny Stories magazine, which had writing competitions in. If I wanted to enter a competition my mother would say, "Don't do that, you will only be disappointed if you don't win." When I was in bed with one of my frequent childhood illnesses, my mother would buy me Lucozade to drink and a bar of Cadbury milk chocolate, and extra books would be fetched from the library. As I got older, I read the News of the World to see the words I wasn't supposed to know about and then I would discuss them at school with friends. We also talked about the pictures of the naked women in the National Geographical magazine. An American serviceman, Bill Kloeblen, who had been billeted at my grandmother's house during the war, sent these to her.

From my mother's bedroom window, I could see a tall pear tree and on the top branch a thrush would sit singing, "pretty dick, pretty dick". I would look at the sky beyond as I lay in bed listening to the sweetness of his song.

At the top of the stairs, to the right, was a bedroom that had two steps down to it. This was my aunt's room, which had a large brass bedstead and a chest of drawers. The woodwork was painted grey and the walls were pink with pretty, flowered curtains at the window. From this window, which had had bars put across it when I was a toddler, I could see into next-door's kitchen. In 1957, when I was 13, my aunt married and left home and I was given her bedroom. I remember waking up in there one night. I was terrified because there was someone bending over me. I suppose it was just a dream, but the black figure I had seen seemed so real.

Nannie cooked and cleaned, but I don't remember her greeting me or making me a cup of tea. I don't have a clear memory of her sitting down and eating with us and yet she was there, all the time. Later in life I learnt that people had found her formidable, but I hadn't. I can remember once

getting into bed with her in the afternoon, but I didn't like
it. Why don't I remember her as a person? She is not in my
wedding pictures, although she attended. I can catch a glimpse
of her on my eldest daughter's christening pictures.

Did I love my grandmother? It is not something I'd have
ever thought about. Bill's widow, Betty told me that she was
afraid of this rather dominating figure. I was never afraid of
her, but I never felt close to her. I was irritated by the fact that
I had to be mindful of the fact it was her house. It gave me an
irritability with old people. As a teenager I resented her and
had little patience with her. If I had a friend round I had to
be quiet from 1pm to 3pm when my grandmother had her
daily rest. I would tiptoe around the house, read a book or
when it was warm enough I would go outside to escape the
quietness. I would throw a rubber ball against the long north
wall, waiting for it to bounce before I caught it. In summer I
would go into the garden, pick rose petals and put them into
jam jars of water to make perfume. I liked going into the large
vegetable garden to dig for pieces of broken china. But once
I was back in the house, the heavy feeling would return. The
words, "It is your grandmother's house," were said to me so
often by my mother.

I was allowed to have a cat. He was black with a white bib
and I called him Timmy. He would curl up in the crook of the
back of my knees when I was in bed. How I loved his warmth
and his purring! I was made aware that this was a tremendous
concession on my grandmother's part. She didn't like animals
as they cost money to feed. Timmy was fed with boiled cods
heads that we got free from the fishmonger every Tuesday and
Saturday. When the heads were being cooked, the kitchen

would fill with fish-scented steam and when cooked the eyes would be enlarged and white. The fish would be gluttonous and sticky and the white lumps of cod would fall easily from the large fish bones. Timmy sometimes had a tin of cat food and was allowed one saucer of milk a day. That would be full cream as semi-skimmed and skimmed milk weren't heard of then. Skimmed milk is just blue milk that's had all the goodness skimmed off.

Later I was allowed a dog. My neighbour's daughter, Phyllis, known as Billy, was a milk lady. She had seen this dog being kicked by the owner and when she had objected, she was told to take the dog with her. So she did. Lifting him up to put him in the milk float, she said, "Why you look just like a bundle of rags," hence Rags became his name. I used to go round to see Rags. Billy's dad didn't want him, so I asked if I could have him and as a great favour I was allowed to have him. He was a good companion and I have many pictures of us together. I think he was a handful for my mother and grandmother. He used to run off whenever he got the scent of a bitch, which was often. Again, dogs were an expense, but by this time Nannie was old and not so spirited.

I was so casual about her, inasmuch as she was just a rather remote old lady. I didn't appreciate her or what she had been through. How could I? I was just a child and I knew nothing about her life at that time. Back then it was thought better not to tell children things to protect them from the harsher side of life. I feel sure that any positive qualities I have, I have inherited from my grandmother. Should I ever meet her again, I would apologise to her for the lack of respect I showed her as I was growing up and I would thank her for all she gave me:

a home, stability, a love of cooking, an ability to cope, to be practical and to get on with life. She had a great toughness of spirit. After she died and as I got older, I came to value her and the stabilising influence she was on my life. But at the time and because of the conflicts in the house – my mother always frightened that my father would turn up and Dah, always critical and disapproving – I kept out of the adults' way as much as possible.

Chapter Three

To me she was Nannie and I am known as Nan to my grandchildren, a name abbreviated and passed down. I asked my grandson Dan what he would remember about me when he was 60. "Your cooking," he said. "Especially your chocolate cake."

***

There was a definite pattern to the meals we ate. All the cooking was done by Nannie; the rabbit stews, the chocolate buns, the little cakes that were called hobney-dobs, which were lumps of cooked sweet pastry with the two halves put together with pink or white icing sugar. When I was an adult I found the recipe in my grandmother's recipe book. I have tried to make them, but they didn't come out the same as I remembered.

On Sunday we had a roast, sometimes pork, but only if there was an r in the month. The reason for this was that those months were cooler months and pork was meat that could go off. There were no fridges in those days, and even when there were, we didn't have one. The meat was kept in the pantry. Pork was served with apple sauce. This would be made either using cooking apples fresh from the garden or apples that had been stored over the winter months. Pork was cooked in lard, which is the way I still do it because I love pork dripping that is poured from the pan after the meat has been roasted. The white dripping would set hard and at the bottom would be a dark, brown jelly. The dripping would be spread onto thick white toast and sprinkled with salt. I still eat toast and dripping. It is the only time that I eat white bread. Bad for me maybe, but my grandmother lived to be 83 and I can never remember her being ill.

The other meat would be lamb or rather mutton, as it was cheaper. This would be served with mint sauce made from mint grown in the garden. I don't remember having beef and chicken was just eaten at Christmas, as it was luxury meat at that time. There would be roast potatoes and Yorkshire pudding, never the buns that are so popular now. Any leftovers of the Yorkshire would be served as a dessert with golden syrup. Delicious! It is still eaten this way in the family. The vegetables with the meal would be something from the garden, but I think there was only ever one vegetable, not a variety as is the fashion today. The sweet would be tinned fruit, either peaches or rings of pineapple served with evaporated milk.

Monday was washday, which took up the best part of the morning so as there was no time for cooking. A fire would be lit under the copper into which water, washing powder, sheets, towels, pillows cases and tea towels would be put and then covered with a wooden lid. When the water boiled the kitchen would fill with steam. When the items had boiled for long enough the washing would be removed by my grandmother with a pair of wooden tongs and put into the sink. This was followed by a great deal of rinsing of the soapy materials, then the wicker basket, heavy with dripping, wet washing, would have been carried out to the shed. A white enamel bucket would be placed under the mangle to catch the water as the clothes went through the wooden rollers.

My grandmother would then lift the washing from the basket, folding it flat. Any buttons would be turned inwards so that they did not break. She would turn the mangle handle, pushing through pale pink knickers with long elasticated legs, thick stockings, pillowcases and the sheets. After she had finished the mangling she would throw the grey soapy water from the bucket out onto the garden. In the winter, her fingers would become icy cold as she pegged the washing out, using wooden pegs which were made using two pieces of wood bound at the top with silver metal, often bought from Gypsies that called round, not the spring-clip pegs we use today. In the afternoon, before it became dark, my grandmother would collect the washing in, knocking off the small particles of fragile ice that would lie in the folds of the clothes and sheets. Indoors, I would take one end of the sheets, holding the white linen tightly whilst my grandmother shook it into shape and then folded it. After it was ironed it would be hung on the wooden clotheshorse around the fire, steam rising, with the smell of the washing soap filling the room. Curled up in a chair near the fire, I would sit drinking my cocoa comforted by the warmth, before going to bed between clean, white sheets.

I remember the silver twisted wire line, strung from apple tree to apple tree that my grandmother hung the washing on. The line was pulled tight around the bark so that it cut deep into the wood. I do not remember the washing hung out on warm days, just on cold frosty days when the frozen sheets would hang like boards.

Because Monday was washday, dinner was cold meat left over from the day before. If mutton had been the meat, the cold leftovers had a large amount of thick white fat on them. I would imagine it was like chewing gum just to be able to eat it. The potatoes with the meal would be baked or mashed.

Tuesday was shepherd's pie day. If we had lamb on Sunday my grandmother would put the leftover meat through a mincer for this dish, otherwise she would buy beef mince from the butcher. The pie would be topped with mashed potato and served with either carrots or if in season, brussel sprouts.

Wednesday's meal of liver was my favourite meal of the week. It would be lambs' liver with fried onions, mashed potatoes and vegetables, usually peas either fresh or tinned, and thick gravy. The pudding, or dessert as it was sometimes called, would be steamed. Liver and fried onions is still one of my favourite meals, although I only cook it for Gary and myself. Offal is not popular with young people. I once asked my granddaughter if she ever ate liver or if she would. "Ugh," she said. "Never." I guess all young people feel the same about offal. When I ate it, I had no idea about where it came from. I just found it delicious.

So, there I was, each Wednesday, a skinny child, sitting at the dining room table waiting for my favourite meal. Two slices of liver served with a pile of fried onions, cooked until they were soft and just turning brown, beside a heap of creamed potatoes and peas, covered in thick gravy. This would be followed by steamed chocolate pudding served with sweet white sauce.

***

On a recent visit to my local butcher I see the liver and buy a pound. I can bypass where it comes from and the fact it is offal. I am back to my childhood. I return home and on a large plate I sprinkle a thick layer of flour and drag the liver through it, so it is covered on both sides. I peel and slice the onions, which I cook in my non-stick frying pan, not the heavy one my grandmother used. I peel the potatoes and put them in the saucepan to cook whilst I cook the onions until they are soft and transparent. Their sweet smell fills the kitchen and childhood memories envelop me.

Now in my kitchen, the potatoes are cooked. I strain and mash them, add butter and milk and then cream them with a wooden spoon. Using a slotted spoon, I scrape the onions from the pan into a bowl before adding the liver to the pan. I turn the gas up high, the floured offal turns brown and in minutes the liver is cooked. Using the flour from the plate, I make the thick gravy and serve the meal onto two white plates. I watch as the steam rises from the potatoes. I carry the plates to the table and call Gary through into the kitchen. As I turn I see a shadow of someone standing by the cooker, but it is just a trick of the light I think, nothing more.

***

Thursday was stew day. Chunks of shin of beef and delicious kidney in thick gravy with onions, and carrots topped with suet dumplings that were brown and crisp on top. Again, served with mashed potatoes and one vegetable, brussel sprouts if available or a tinned vegetable.

Friday's meal was pork sausages with fried onions, thick gravy and mashed potatoes. Saturday was fish day with the fish being bought from the stall on the market. Framlingham is a small market town, famous now because of Ed Sheeran. The centre is called Market Hill and is surrounded by shops. There has been a market of sorts on there since the year dot. Tuesday's market is smaller, fish and veg normally, but the Saturday market has grown over the years. The choice of fish back then was cod, plaice or haddock. Sometimes the fishmonger, David, would have kippers, herrings and/or bloaters. In the shrimp season there would be piles of pink and brown shrimps that would be bought in pint measures, peeled and used as a filling for sandwiches for tea. The vegetable with the fish was always peas, tinned or fresh, depending on the season. Then frozen peas became available. They would be bought just before lunchtime from Mrs Steggall's grocery store on Market Hill along with an ice cream for the pudding that was kept wrapped in newspaper, so it didn't melt before it could be eaten.

I always had a glass of water with my meals. I had choked on a hard sweet at the age of nine. My aunt hooked the sweet with her fingers, but scarred my throat in the doing of it. For two years I ate very little. I was too scared. I always had to have water when I ate a meal and I still do.

There were variations with the puddings that we would have each day. A favourite of mine was lemon meringue pie, such a luxury. It always seemed to me to be a party sort of pudding. My grandmother made it using a packet mix, which had the word Royal on the front of the box. Rice pudding, semolina and apple crumble were others. Treacle tart was another favourite, which would be served with custard. Banana custard was made using over-ripe bananas that would be sliced and custard would be poured over them. When cool the banana custard would be topped with a small amount of grated chocolate and chopped up glace cherries. Another pudding was flummery. This was whisked evaporated milk, which would then be added to a nearly set raspberry jelly, a sort of melt in the mouth pink mousse. If it was raspberry season it would be topped with raspberries from the garden. Sometimes a pink blancmange would appear on the table in the shape of a rabbit, the mixture having been poured into a rabbit-shaped tin. There were fruit pies using the fruit that was in season in the garden; apples, blackcurrants or gooseberries and stewed rhubarb served with delicious sweet condensed milk. I enjoyed dipping a teaspoon in the tin when no one was looking. Steamed puddings were a great filler; jam, treacle or suet jam roll poly or spotted dick. The latter would be made with suet, flour, water and sultanas. The meals we had echoed the way life was at that time, routine, the same day in and day out. When my grandmother made jam tarts, she would use the leftover pastry, which would be rolled and filled with sugar and currants, topped with more pastry and brushed with egg before being criss-crossed on top with a knife before going into the oven to bake. When cooked, it would be cut into small squares.

The cooking was done in the kitchen, a room I remember with great clarity. There was a brick floor, the bricks were stone-coloured and partially covered with a course piece of coco matting. In the corner was a built-in copper that was filled with water, under which a fire would be lit to heat the water to boil the washing in. I can remember the scum on the water and the big round wooden lid that covered it. I have

memories of getting washed in the kitchen with water that
had been boiled in the kettle and put into a bowl in the sink
on freezing cold mornings before the small oil heater had a
chance to warm the kitchen. On bath night, a fire would be
lit under the water-filled copper, then the long, galvanised tin
bath that hung on a hook outside in the yard would be bought
in and the hot water from the copper poured in from a jug.
After bathing in about three inches of not very hot water, my
mother then had the job of emptying it, jug full by jug full.

The sink in the kitchen was shallow and made of brown
stone with a cold water tap above it. On the windowsill was
a dish containing soap and flannels. There was a mantelshelf
above a chimneybreast. It served no purpose except that on it
was kept a mug with toothbrushes in and a small, coloured,
round tin, inside which was a pink tablet of Gibb's Dentifrice
that would be rubbed with a wetted toothbrush to make the
paste for teeth cleaning.

There were a few utensils in the kitchen. In the drawer
of a small wooden table there was a wooden spoon, a knife
and knife sharpener, metal spoons, a tin opener, numerous
meat skewers and string. Somehow though with so little, my
grandmother managed to produce amazing meals. Everything
was cooked on the small grey and white gas cooker with its
four legs that lifted it off the bricks. It had the word MAIN in
capital letters on the front.

Since the kitchen table was too small to eat at, meals were
served in the dining room. It was cosy, especially in winter when
a daily fire was lit. There was a wicker chair made by a local
basket maker in front of the fire and in the winter a wooden
clotheshorse, used for airing clothes on, would be folded out

around it. Fixed onto the fire grate was a small metal plate on which a kettle stood, always filled with water to boil to make tea. Hanging on a hook nearby was a knitted square with which to hold the hot handle of the kettle. In a photograph album there are pictures of me being bathed in a small, oval tin bath in front of that fire. The pictures are in black and white, but looking at the photo I can feel the warmth of the flickering flames.

In the dining room was an oak sideboard. A homemade red rug lay by the fireplace and the floor was covered with dark red and blue linoleum. Cupboards were built into the recesses on either side of the fireplace. These contained books, games, tablemats and pieces of material, plates, wool, china, towels and tea towels. On the narrow shelf above the fireplace there was a clock and two jugs containing scissors and pencils and "odds and ends" as my grandmother put it. In the 1950s there wasn't television and advertising on the scale there is today so to me, this room was just like everyone else's. In the few houses I went into I found that the dining rooms were just variations of ours and were rooms that served a useful purpose.

The dining table, which was squeezed in under the window, had two leaves that could be pulled out when we had company. There were five matching chairs plus a grandfather chair with side arms. My grandmother had bought it with her husband when they married in 1907. When I was first married I had the table and chairs at my home. It then went to Sarah, my oldest daughter. Now her family and my grandchildren sit around it. If I eat with her, as we go to sit down, she will raise her eyebrows as if to say, "Don't mention the bloody table, Mother!" I do tend to bring it into conversation. I might over the years have

mentioned the small grooves made with a fountain pen when
I did my homework or my memories of sitting around it as a
child, but nowadays I obey the raised eyebrows.

A small room leading off from the kitchen was called
the back place. It was half the width of the kitchen and it
backed onto the wall of the outdoor lavatory. The back place
was where all the oddments were kept. There were piles of
newspapers, a box with dusters in and a tin of black boot
polish and brushes to clean the shoes with. Brooms and
furniture polish were kept here in a wooden box and behind
the door hung aprons and a red leather homemade bag in
which string and sealing wax was kept. The brick walls were
white washed with distemper and the floor was uneven yellow
brick. Large spiders that my mother called Horaces, lived
amongst the dust. There was a small window with a single
pane in that overlooked the garden and the tiny square of
grass. The door of the back place was made of four dark wood
panels with a brass bolt on to fasten the door.

***

A rough, narrow concrete path led down to the back door of
number 13. On one side was the outside loo adjoining the red
bricks of the house. On the other was the long, wooden coal
shed with a corrugated tin roof. The door into the dusty, dark
shed was narrow and adults had to bend down to get inside. The
coal would be emptied from sacks, delivered and carried in on
the back of the coal man, his face ingrained with the black dust.

A short-handled metal shovel lay just inside the shed
entrance. This was used to shovel the coal into a tin bucket

that was taken inside for the fire. A lump hammer, used to
break up the larger pieces of coal, lay beside it. I didn't mind
filling the bucket when the coal had just been delivered. But
I did not like it when stocks were low and I had to go to the
back of the shed, bending over and feeling the thick cobwebs
against my face. On the right-hand side of the door was a
smaller space where the logs and bikes were kept.

In the cold days of winter when it snowed, I would look out
of the small kitchen window and see the snow piled up on the
coal shed roof. As the snow thawed, dripped down and froze
again, a line of long, glass-like icicles would form. I would
watch the slow drips of water falling into slushy melting snow.

I don't have a picture of the coal shed, just the space where
it once was, where now against the wall, a straggling, purple
clematis climbs.

Against the shed, to one side, was an iron pump from which
my grandmother got water before the water mains were laid.
Against the back wall of the house, where the outside loo
was, there was a deep groove of damp earth where lilies of the
valley grew.

***

Nothing was wasted. My grandmother kept everything she
thought might be useful. String was rolled up into small balls
and brown paper that parcels came in smoothed and folded
up: "Just in case," my grandmother would say. The paper that
wrapped the packs of block margarine would be used as covers
for the steamed puddings. The paper bags that the bread and
other wrapped groceries came in were folded and put into the

drawer of the kitchen table along with the meat skewers and other odds and ends. Flannels and dusters would be used and boiled clean until they were threadbare. When soap got down to a small piece it would be wetted with other saved pieces and then pushed and kneaded together to be used and used again.

In the winter we went sticking, as collecting firewood was called. The thin sticks would be put into a large, red, suede bag that my grandmother had made. We would walk through the woods and pick up pieces that had fallen from the trees that could be used for firewood.

Cooking fat was never tipped away, but used until there were more black bits in it than fat. Stale bread that was too far gone even for toast, would be used to make bread and butter pudding. The rest would be toasted and rolled into crumbs that would be placed into a screw topped jar and saved to be used to rub on the outside of the hams my grandmother cooked. Rinds would be trimmed off the bacon before cooking and these would be tied together with string and hung from a branch of the apple tree for birds to enjoy.

Socks were darned using a wooden darning mushroom pushed into the heel of the sock. I still have the darning mushroom that was used by my grandmother. Old stockings that were beyond darning were used to tie on to the end of drainpipes that went down into the soft water butt to catch any sludge and prevent it from entering the water. When clothes were beyond repair they were put into the ragbag that hung on a hook on the back place door. These would be used for polishing cloths until there was nothing but a small piece of material left.

My grandmother was not alone in her in ability not to waste

anything. People consumed much less food then and there was less food wrapping and pre-packed food. For this reason, there wasn't much rubbish. We had a grey metal dustbin kept around the back of the house, which the bin men came in their dust-cart every Monday to collect. A bin man would hoist the bin onto his shoulder and tip the contents into the cart. The cart had three metal sliding panels on each side and they would be opened one at a time for the rubbish to be tipped into.

I do remember we had two new coco matting doormats. These were put down near the back door to replace the ones worn away with the wiping of feet. Just before I left home in 1963, my grandmother received a grant to have a bathroom put in and the back place became a bathroom. When I married, our first home, which was rented, did not have a bathroom or hot water, so I would go to number 13 for a bath. I had never imagined that room being anything else. Years later, when I returned to the house, the bathroom had been moved, this time up into the bedroom where I had slept as a child. The kitchen was now one large room with a large picture window overlooking the small landscaped garden. There was no trace of the back place, the outside lavatory or the old bathroom.

***

Suffolk Rusks (Nannie Nicholls)

8oz hard (block) margarine
1lb self raising flour
2 eggs beaten with a little milk

Pinch of salt if desired

Mix together sieved flour and margarine using finger tips. When well 'crumbed', add milk and eggs and mix to a pliable dough. Roll out to a good 1 inch to 1.5 inches. Using a circular cutter cut into the dough and place the cut rusks on to a greased baking sheet.

Put into a pre-heated oven, gas mark 6 or 7 for 10 minutes, then remove and cut in half, using either a fork or knife. Return the separated rusks to the oven for a further 10 to 15 minutes, until the rusks are golden brown on top and fairly dry. Transfer the rusks onto a cooling tray.

***

Suffolk rusks are a peculiarity to Suffolk. It seems they never go beyond the border of this county. They were a recipe of my grandmother's, which I still use. I don't put salt in the mixture and I use self-raising flour. It is a simple recipe to make, a bit like scone mixture without the sugar, although I did see it in a local magazine once with sugar added; tut tut, not the Suffolk way at all. As I said, it is a bit like making scones, only the rusks are cut in half, half way through cooking, or forked in half, which is how my grandmother used to do it. They are then returned to the oven and cooked until the tops are brown and they are cooked through. When taken out of the oven they are left to cool before being eaten with butter and a bit of cheese and celery. My grandchildren like them with strawberry jam and I like them spread with Marmite or Bovril. For me, the latter is the best, with a thick layer of butter put on first.

One word of warning, if there are folks in the kitchen when the rusks are taken out of the oven there will be no time for them to cool. The rusks will be taken from the tray, spread with butter and eaten whilst warm, just delicious. It is the Suffolk way.

Chapter Four

I wasn't allowed to eat between meals, although I was given
a glass of milk and a biscuit mid-morning for my elevenses.
Meal times were called breakfast, dinner, and tea. The midday
meal that I have written about was always called dinner. For
supper I had a mug of hot milk and two biscuits before I
went to bed. Breakfasts were porridge or cereal and toast,
sometimes with eggs and bacon, and tea consisted of bread
and butter with jam and cake. I cannot remember who would
get the breakfast, but the oak table in the dining room was
always laid up for that meal before my grandmother went
to bed each night. The butter dish would be stood in the
fireplace until the butter was softened and then it would be
mixed with margarine, to make the butter go further.

My grandmother made and cooked everything herself and
whenever I could, I watched her. She did buy some things
though such as little chocolate cupcakes with thick chocolate
icing that were in a case of ridged silver paper. And tea cakes,
those chocolate covered marshmallow cakes which have jam
underneath the marshmallow. Unlike Nannie, my mother was
not a good cook. Later, when she was on her own, she seemed
to live on fish fingers and things I made for her, although she
made very good shortbread and marmalade.

As a child I always had to eat my crusts because I was told this would make my hair curly. I don't eat crusts now for as I pointed out to someone who said I should, "I am all grown up and if I want to leave them, I can."

My biggest treat when I was young was being allowed to have my tea in the garden. It had to be a hot day and the ground had to be dry. My mother fussed a lot. I had to have a groundsheet put down first, covered by a blanket before I was allowed to sit on the grass. Tea was always a tomato sandwich, a chocolate Kit Kat and a glass of milk from a glass bottle that had been delivered by the milkman. The best thing about eating outside was that I could read whilst I ate, usually one of the Famous Five books written by Enid Blyton.

***

The flames flicker in the dining room fireplace and small sparks catch against the black soot in the chimney. I am drinking mushroom soup from a large china mug. I have a spoon to scoop out the small pieces of mushroom that will be left in the bottom when I have drunk the thick, pale brown liquid.

The three-sided wooden clotheshorse that is near the fire is hung with ironed bed linen to finish drying. The heat on the smooth white sheets makes a warm smell that is mingled with washing powder. I am sitting on a wicker basket-weave chair that has a circular supporting bottom and a high wooden back that curves around me. A local basket weaver, Jack Daines of Dennington, made it. There is an identical-in-style, much smaller chair beside me. I would use it for my doll to sit in, but I have grown out of playing with dolls and now my black and white cat, Timmy, is curled up in it, his tail and one paw hang over the edge of the seat. On both of the chairs there is a cushion. The doll that once sat in that seat is called Patsy. She now sits on the bookcase in my bedroom. Her arms and legs are held in place by thick elastic and hooks inside the body of the doll. The brown wig on her head is made from real hair and was acquired when the doll went to the doll's hospital to be mended after the elastic had frayed and snapped. I liked Patsy better without hair.

Years later, after I left home and married, I asked my mother where Patsy was. "I put her in the dustbin when you left home," my mother replied. I thought of Patsy in her pink and blue flowered dress, wig askew, tipped into the rubbish and covered in ash. I wondered why my mother had been so brutal. I didn't ask, but just shrugged my shoulders and turned away.

I push my spoon to the bottom of the mug and scoop up the small pieces of mushroom. Then lifting the mug to my lips, I drink the remaining liquid. I finish drinking the mushroom soup and sit curled up in the chair, one leg folded back under my bottom. I am wearing a pair of patterned, flannel, dark pink pyjamas, which were a Christmas present from my grandmother. I had been given two pairs. The other pair was blue. It was the same present every year. Forever afterwards I always associated new pyjamas with Christmas.

***

It is funny thing, memory. It can make one remember things that didn't happen, gloss over or distort things that did and can be triggered off by the slightest thing; the smell of grass, the long shadows of a summer's evening, a soft spring breeze, the smell of ripe blackberries. Any of these can take me right back to that summer of long ago when things were perfect. Was there such a summer?

My grandmother is cooking in the kitchen. She is a tall, well-built woman, with grey hair pinned back into a knot at the back of her neck. The cooking is done in a small gas oven beside which stands a table, sprinkled with flour on which to roll pastry. Today's lunch is rabbit pie with thick brown onion gravy. I just need to be wary of pieces of shot.

I am five years old. I have thick blonde pigtails tied with large pink bows. I remember standing in the doorway, feeling the warmth of the kitchen and the smell of cooking. A batch of freshly baked chocolate buns stands on the table. On seeing me, my Grandmother smiles.

"Here," she says, "have one. I know you like them when they've just come out of the oven."

My grandmother gives me a glass of milk to drink with the chocolate bun. I can still remember how delicious they were.

***

I feel the warmth of her kitchen and smell the cooking smells when I bake chocolate buns and pies and stews. I can see again my grandmother cooking meals and I smile to myself and think how the essence of her grandmother lives through her actions and memories. I made some chocolate buns for my best friend Daphne once.

"Lovely," she said. "I'll freeze them for another day."

I told her that they wouldn't taste the same as eaten fresh, but she froze them anyway.

Chapter Five

Christmas Day is a special day for food and was the same during my childhood. At Christmas, my grandmother came into her own with the cooking of the chicken lunch. The chicken weighed 12lbs so I am not sure how it fitted into the oven. The night before Christmas there would be stuffing to make. That would be put into the front of the bird and then the flap would be sewn up with a needle and strong white thread. Nowadays it is considered dangerous to do this as the food juices can run into the stuffing and can cause food poisoning, but there weren't so many dos and don'ts in those days. The small kitchen would be hot and steamy. My grandmother would wear a long, homemade pinafore over her best Sunday clothes. I was always impatient for lunch to be under way because after we had eaten I would be allowed to open my remaining presents. I had of course had my stocking presents to open when I had woken in the morning.

The only foods I can remember eating with the chicken were sprouts, stuffing and bread sauce. Following this would be a homemade Christmas pudding with a silver sixpence in. I always found the sixpence, but I now realise that the little silver coin was pushed into my pudding as it was served. It was such a treat to eat food that was not readily available throughout the year. Bottles of drinks would be ordered from the local wine merchant, Carley and Webb, and delivered just before the 25th. They would be stood on top of the piano and on Christmas Day I would be given a glass of lime juice mixed with soda from the soda siphon.

For tea on Christmas Day we had cheese from the local grocer, which I now know was cheddar, and celery with white bread and butter. The celery was dug up from the garden and the crisp white stalks were scrubbed and washed to remove the brown earth. The top green leaves were chopped off with the long stalks sliced and placed in a glass jug. The bottom of the celery was more solid and different to the main stalks. It was what my grandmother referred to as the nutty part, and it was the bit I enjoyed most. Shop bought celery nowadays lacks the taste and crispness of the celery that was grown by my grandmother.

After celery and cheese we had Christmas cake covered with hard white icing and decorated with blobs of pink icing around the edge. On the top were small decorations of artificial holly, a robin, a Christmas tree and a Father Christmas that had yellowed with age. Somehow amongst all that, the words Happy Christmas were piped on in thick pink ribbon icing. The finishing touch was the shiny red and white frill that was wrapped around the cake.

As I got older, after the Christmas tea we would play cards in the dining room. The 'we' consisted of my grandmother, my mother and Dah. I was given a little drawstring purse with pennies in for this event. Newmarket was the favourite game with Seven's being a close second. Years later my mother told me that the cards were fixed so I could win. I was not amused by this revelation.

After the Christmas lunch and when the washing up was done, I would walk down the dark, narrow hallway into the front room where the tall, decorated pine Christmas tree was in the bay window. The copper tray and table on which the maiden-hair fern stood for the rest of the year would have been moved into my grandmother's bedroom.

Paper decorations hung from the ceiling. The branches of the tree were hung with purple and silver baubles in which I would see my distorted reflection. There were silver coloured candleholders, which held small red candles and were clipped onto the end of each branch. These were lit on Christmas Day evening, but they had to be watched just in case they set light to the tree. There would be a fire in the grate and the flames would light the room. I always thought it was the best fire of the year. In that room was a three-piece-suite that was covered with a harsh, pale brown, ridged material. The settee would be pulled up close to the fire and I would watch as small golden sparks clung to the soot of the chimney. In the coals of the fire we would roast chestnuts or soften pink and white marshmallows in the heat on a long toasting fork. I would sit in what I regarded as a magical place just for a brief time of the year.

I would then open my presents. These would be a School Friend's annual, a book written by Enid Blyton and pencils and pens. One year I unwrapped a present from my grandmother. Inside the wrapping there was a small silver coloured tin and when I opened it a handful of three-penny bits fell out. I remember my grandmother smiling at me, but I had hoped for something more exciting.

As I opened my gifts, I would feel the warmth of the fire

on my legs. Then it would be time to light the candles. "Be careful," my aunt would say, a slight disapproving tone in her voice. My mother would smile and strike a match and my aunt would join in and one by one the candles would bring the tree to life. I would watch as the small flames were reflected in the shining baubles. In the top branch of the tree was the fairy. She had brown hair and a crown made of tinsel. Her wand was a matchstick covered in silver paper with a homemade star stuck onto it. Her dress was made from a creamy white satin and her wings, formed from muslin and wire with a silver star on each of them, seemed to move in the candle flames. I remember when the Christmas Fairy had arrived. She had come as an ordinary doll wrapped up in a brown paper parcel as a present from my father. He'd had no contact with me and my mother didn't want me to keep the doll, but then I found a use for it; so every Christmas his gift appeared. I liked that.

On the evenings after Christmas while the tree was still up, we continued to spend our evenings in the front room. Bread would be toasted by the fire and spread with pork dripping and sprinkled with salt. It was cosy, but the cold that came in under the door and through the ill-fitting windows cut into the back of my legs while the fire burned the front of them. Chestnuts were bought at Christmas time. Their brown skins would be pricked and the nuts would be placed in the ashes of the fire and roasted until the skins were black and hard. These would be snapped off to reveal black burnt flesh on one side and yellow on the other. The nut would then be dipped in salt and eaten.

The next day the long empty days after Christmas would begin. My best friend Daphne who lived on the road had five sisters, but I was an only child, living with my mother, aunt and grandmother. Daphne and my other friends were busy with their family so the days after Christmas dragged along until we could all meet up again.

Chapter Six

Away From Home – An imagining based on truth

Ada wondered about Tom, her husband, who was out in the trenches in France. She couldn't imagine France. She had been told it was a bit like England, but of course the people spoke differently. She wondered what Tom was doing. She looked out of the window at her three children playing hide-and-seek in the garden. William aged nine, tall and wearing glasses, was a solemn boy. "Look after your sisters," Tom had said to him, "and your mother whilst I'm gone." William took his responsibilities very seriously.

Then there was Gladys aged seven, a quiet child with straight, brown hair and large, dark eyes, who didn't mention her father very often and Mary aged six, who was devoted to William. She was a lively child with blonde, wavy hair and bright, blue eyes. Every day she would ask her mother, "When is Daddy coming home? It won't be long will it?" William would nudge her and tell her to "shush" because he knew it upset his mother.

Ada turned away from the window. It was a hot summer's day. The voices of her children calling, "Ready!" "Come and find me!" and "You can't have counted to 100 already!"

floated towards her. She had sewing to do for a neighbour
who wanted a long skirt and cape made for the winter. But
sitting at the square oak table that Tom had bought when
they married, she found it hard to concentrate and the thick
black material stuck to the sweat of her hands. She turned the
handle of the sewing machine and watched the needle going
up and down and in and out of the material as it made small
stitches. The rhythm of it soothed her.

She thought of the other women in her street whose sons
and husbands were in France. They all had the same fear, that
their men might not return, but she told herself daily that
Tom would come back. Tom and the others from the village
had gone off together to the sound of a brass band playing.
A crowd of locals had turned out to watch them as they
marched to the local railway station. Ada had stood, her back
as straight as a ramrod with her three children beside her. As
the train pulled out, Tom had waved and Ada had waved back.
Others around her were weeping, but she wasn't too given to
public emotion.

She'd caught Tom's words as he called through the window
of the train, "I'll be back." She'd nodded, waved, watched until
the train disappeared from view and then turned and walked
home. She'd entered the empty house telling herself it was just
as if Tom had gone to work, only he would be away a little bit
longer. That was all.

She finished sewing the seam of the skirt and removed
the material from the machine. Looking up, she saw Mary
running down the yard and seconds later she was in the room.
"They found me Mummy and I'm tired of hide and seek.
When will Daddy be home?"

Ada took Mary's hand. "As soon as he can," she said. "I'll make some sandwiches and we'll have a picnic in the garden." Then she added, "I expect Daddy is eating some food outside somewhere in France. William! Gladys!"

The children helped their mother prepare the food and carry it, together with a groundsheet and rugs, into the garden. There was an apple tree in the corner of the lawn. They sat underneath it and for a while Ada was distracted from thoughts of Tom, but then she looked at the faces of the children and wished that there wasn't a war.

William was watching wasps in a jam jar. Ada had made a wasp catcher by putting some of her homemade raspberry jam into a jar and mixing it with water. She had tied a thick piece of brown paper on the top and made holes in it which were big enough for the wasps to get in but not out again. The jar was kept on the windowsill by the back door but William had taken it into the garden to watch the thick layer of wasps climbing on each other's backs as they tried to get out of the sticky water.

Gladys gathered rose petals from the creamy pink Albertine rose that Tom had planted when William was born. It had grown well and was now trailing along the outside hedge. She put the petals into a jar and added water to make rose petal scent. The petals had turned brown. Gladys took the lid off the jar and gave it to her mother to smell. "Put some behind your ears, Mummy," she said. Ada dipped her fingers into the warm water and dabbed her ears as instructed. "It's the best scent ever," she said, giving Gladys a hug.

Mary snuggled up to her mother, her thumb in her mouth.

"I think," Ada said, "that it's time that you three children had a rest for half an hour and whilst you're doing that I'll pick some fruit from the garden."

She watched the children go indoors before going to the large black garden shed. She collected two wicker baskets and, walking out to the vegetable garden where the fruit bushes grew, began to gather gooseberries. She wore a straw hat to protect herself from the sun and could feel small beads of perspiration on her face. When she had picked all the gooseberries she went over to the blackcurrant bushes and her fingers became stained from the dark red juice of the fruit.

Ada had a wild rabbit indoors that a local farmer had shot and given to her. She was going to skin it and make rabbit pie and a blackcurrant pie with fruit from the garden for the day after. She thought about how much Tom would have enjoyed her rabbit pie with its golden crust and served with thick gravy. It was one of his favourites. She carried the fruit into the shed and then walked out into the garden and stood amongst the tall red gladioli and Sweet Williams that grew alongside the onion bed. She looked to the top of the garden where there was a plum tree and greengage tree. The fruit was nearly ripe enough to pick. "William could help me do that," she said to herself. "He would enjoy that."

Despite the heat, Ada felt herself shiver. She must go indoors. All this heat wasn't good for her. She didn't want to get heat stroke. She walked along the path and looked down the dusty road. In the distance she saw the postman doing his afternoon rounds. Maybe there would be a letter for her. She hadn't heard from Tom for a while but she knew it was hard for letters to get through from France. She heard her gate click and stood watching as the postman walked towards her. In his hand he held a brown envelope.

"Telegram for you Mrs. Nicholls," he said.

Ada took the brown envelope and opened it before going indoors. Inside, she sat in the cool of the dining room, her elbows resting on the oak table. Looking again at the words of the telegram she moved her arm, and the black material she was working on earlier slipped to the floor.

There was no noise from the children upstairs. They were asleep. When they wake up, Ada thought, I will tell them that their father is not coming home.

***

My mother told me that the memory of my grandfather going off to war was the reason that my grandmother would not go and watch the annual Framlingham Gala Parade since it was led by a brass band.

"She cannot stand to hear it as it brings back too many memories," my mother said.

However, I do remember one occasion. It was when I was a teenager. My grandmother, as an old lady, came to the bottom of the road to watch the parade go past. She had stood very straight. Her hair was grey now and her face lined. It was a cold day. I thought it was the wind that had made my grandmother's eyes water.

***

One thing I did not inherit from my grandmother was her love of gardening. She loved her garden, the big garden,

which was the part furthest from the house. I have a coloured
photograph of her in her garden. It was taken by an American
serviceman during the war. She is standing beside a row
of sweet peas in flower. I had observed her growing them
from seed, and in the picture she is cutting a bunch to bring
indoors. There were always cut flowers in the house in
summer. A dusky pink low bowl, that had an iridescent sheen
like the colour of bubbles that children blow, would be filled
with roses from the garden. At other times it would be filled
with pale pink Albertine roses, bright cerise pink American
Pillar or the old, sweet smelling moss roses that grew in the
privet hedge round the vegetable garden.

In the smaller garden nearer to the house, which was divided
from the big garden by a fence, there were wide flowerbeds,
with pink phlox growing through the hard summer earth and
straggly yellow daisies. Near the wall of the house grew lilies of
the valley. Just by mentioning them I can recall their fragrance.
I have tried to grow them, but without success. In my mind's
eye I can see the strawberry bed and its protective brown net.
This was stretched over the top, supported from the bed by
sticks with jam jars on top. The job of the jars was to stop the
sticks making holes in the net. Any holes had been mended
with string. In the early morning I would go out and untangle
birds that had got trapped in the net.

There was a washing line with dark purple iris' growing
nearby. In the appropriate season my grandmother would
go out at night and sprinkle salt around these flowers. The
following day she would go out with a galvanized tin bucket
to collect the fat black slugs that lay there having perished of a
salty death.

***

Over the years I wrote many pieces about my grandmother; some factual, some imagined, such as this piece below. The garden was real, this is how it was through the seasons. My grandmother's actions are real to me.

It is high summer and the garden is dust dry. There are large cracks in the dry brown soil, where withered roots lay. My grandmother is in her beloved garden. She is wearing a blue dress and a large straw hat and she is picking the ripe yellow gooseberries. Every now and again she puts her finger to her mouth to moisten it and ease the pricks from the short yellow spikes of the gooseberry bush. Small pinhead drops of blood show on her arms. The blood hardens and turns black in the hot sun. She fills her basket with the fruit and then goes to the black wooden shed in the corner of the garden where she lays the basket down. She picks up another basket and a small three-legged stool and makes her way to the blackcurrant bushes. Placing the stool onto the ground, she sits to gather the black fruit and her fingers became stained purple from their juice.

Beside the currant bushes, trails of sweet peas climb up against thin brown canes. A few flowers remain; colours of white and pink, mauve and purples and reds, and amongst the flowers there are small pale green seed pods covered with a soft white fur. There is a scent of roses that comes from the moss roses that grow in the hedge, one pink and one white. The blooms have bright yellow centres and the petals are multi layered.

Narrow paths are laid between vegetable beds and my grandmother, having finished picking the blackcurrants, makes her way to the tall canes where the bright green runner beans grow. She calls them scarlet runners. There are still a few scarlet flowers amongst the leaves. She places her basket of blackcurrants down and picks up a small bag that hangs from the first cane. She walks beside the green plants gathering the long beans as she does so. Camouflaged by the leaves they are difficult to see and she retraces her steps to find the ones she has missed. She leaves the beans that are too hard and long for eating. She will gather them later and break them open and take out the mauve and black marbled beans that she will be plant for next years' crop.

Behind the beans are the large white onions she has harvested. She has tied back their long, dried shoots with orange string and hung them on a pole to finish drying. She walks back to the shed and glancing about she sees the seared grass and the summer crops that have finished for the season. There is dust on her brown laced up shoes and a bead of sweat above her top lip.

Autumn comes. The early morning mists make a pleasant change from the heat of the summer. Now I will help her in her garden. I climb the ladder into the fruit trees to pick the ripe apples and pears and the dark red plums, some half eaten by wasps. My grandmother will make a pie with the plums and serve it with pale yellow custard, which she will share with me. The rest of the fruit she will use to make jam, which will be stored on her high pantry shelf beside the jelly she made from her blackcurrants. The pears she will bottle in large Kilner jars. She will pick over the apples and lay them on brown paper in her loft leaving a gap between each apple so that if one goes bad its soggy brown patch will not infect any other apples.

During the night it has rained and softened the earth. It is time to dig over the garden so the soil can break up and rest, ready to be planted out again. She will check that the celery trench she dug and lined with old newspapers and planted out in June is moist enough and that the plants are growing well. She will think of Christmas time as she does this and the crisp white celery stalks with the nutty root that she will eat with a piece of strong cheese for her Christmas tea. When she has finished she will go to her shed and tidy her tools ready for the spring. The shed has an earth floor and in the corner is an old mangle that was still in use until two years ago. The bucket still stands under the mangle, but now she has a spin dryer. She bought it after an unexpected win with a one-pound premium bond that her daughter had given her. Her winnings were 25 pounds, the exact cost of the spin dryer. Around the shed there are nails in the wood from which string and baskets filled with seed packets and strawberry nets hang. On the floor there are galvanised buckets, glass cloches with their long metal fasteners, stacks of different sized earthenware flower pots, a half empty packet of slug pellets and wooden handled tools, some beyond repair, but not thrown out. Dusty jam jars stand on the shelves some filled with nails, some with pieces of string and in one of them there is salt to put an end to slugs and snails.

It is winter now. The earth is hardened by the frost. There are icicles hanging from the side of the shed. As the days pass, a blanket of snow covers the garden. She looks out of her bedroom window that is frosted inside with ice. She sees the snow and hears the wind howling down the chimney. She goes outside to the coal shed and fills her coal scuttle. Carrying it indoors she places it by the fire and heaps some of the black coal onto the flames. She watches as small pieces of black soot glow orange on the back of the chimney.

She has made a loaf of white bread and she slices off two pieces. She goes to the pantry and takes down a jar of the blackcurrant jelly, which she puts onto a tray with the bread. She then goes through into the sitting room where she takes the butter dish from the hearth. The butter has softened. She places the bread onto a toasting fork, which she holds near the fire. When the bread is toasted she spreads it with the butter and watches as it melts into the toast. She adds the jam and sits warming herself by the fire as she eats.

Later she goes into the garden. She planted out brussel sprouts in May and the now tall stalks poke out and lean at odd angles through the snow. From a stalk she cuts off eight of the small green sprouts and places them in the colander she is carrying. She has left a fork speared into the ground and with effort she manages to dig up one thick, white leek that was planted at the same time as the sprouts. She flicks small white crystals of frost from its green top.

Beside the path is a small upturned tin bath. She carries it over to a patch of earth where there are small shoots of rhubarb hidden in the snow and she places the tin bath over the shoots. She enjoys a moment's pleasure thinking of the bright pink rhubarb that will be forced through and ready to eat in May.

The snow has melted. In the early morning she hears a thrush singing from the top branch of the old pear tree. She dresses and after breakfast she goes into the garden. Small shoots of green are showing through the dark earth and the white snowdrops show their buds. In the corner of the garden there is one yellow aconite. She smiles knowing that spring is on the way.

The hedges burst into green leaf and a light spring rain falls. She smells the earth and the warmth. She watches as the thrush flies into the hedge and she knows that in a month's time there will be a nest with bright turquoise blue, black spotted eggs in. The days begin to pull out. Along the garden hedgerow there are purple violets and the buds of the pale yellow primroses. She opens the shed door and takes out a wooden dibbler to make the holes in the earth for seedlings. She has a line attached to two pieces of pointed metal that she pushes into the ground. She plants a row of broad beans and a row of carrots that she covers with glass cloches. She sorts through her seed potatoes. Good Friday is early this year, which is when the early potatoes are always planted. They are harvested on Whit Monday.

She glances at the strawberry bed. In a month's time it will need straw around the plants and netting to keep the birds off. She hopes there will not be too much rain when the fruit starts to ripen. She thinks of the sweet red fruit and smiles to herself. Soon it will be high summer.

***

Now when I go out into the garden to pick flowers or gather vegetables, I think of my grandmother and remember those hot days of long ago in her garden.

William Crane, my grandmother's grandfather.

My grandmother's parents, Thomas and Emma Crane.

Nannie, pregnant with Bill, with her husband Tom, outside No 17. Aunt Emma is seated.

Tom Nicholls with Auntie Kitty, August 12, 1910.

Tom Nicholls.

Dah, Bill, my mother and Aunt Emma (seated).

Nannie Nicholls (aged approximately 21).

Tom Nicholls (love the writing on this card at the bottom).

Kit, Alice and Ada Crane (seated). Known as the Three Graces.

Nannie (Ada Crane with her three children, Bill, Mary (my mother) and Dah (seated).

Mary (my mother), Bill and Gladys (Dah).

Gladys (Dah), Bill and Mary (my mother).

My mother, aged 21.

Nannie with Jane (me), aged ten months.
Christmas Day 1944.

Nannie with her three grandchildren, Anne,
Pip and Jane (me), aged 2. We are sitting on a
haystack.

Nannie with her three grandchildren, Jane (me),
aged 4, Pip and Anne in the garden of No 13.

Cousins at Thorpeness, Pip, Anne and Jane, 1947.

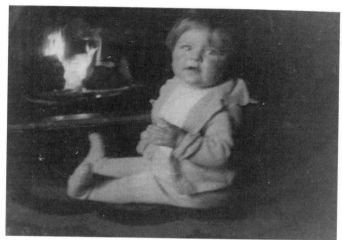

Me, Jane, aged 9 months, sitting in front of the fire after a bath.

My mother and Nannie. My mother would have been about 18 or 21.

Nannie in her garden picking gladioli.

Christmas Day, 1944.

My mother with me on my christening day, aged 5 months and 8 days.

My mother and me.

Nannie in the garden with her Sweet Peas, her favourite flower.

Nannie in Woodland Avenue, Northampton. It was taken in 1962. She died in September, 1965 aged 83. A very fine lady.

Chapter Seven

There was a shop across the road from my grandmother's house. Bonney's Bakers, it was called. Stanley Bonney was a small, slender man with skin the colour of the white flour that he baked with. He always wore a flour-covered apron covering his dusty clothes. I would say he was old, but as a child most adults seemed old to me. Stanley Bonney delivered his bread from a large wicker basket carried on one arm. His daily saying was, "Bonney's Bread is Best."

There was another baker in the shop, a tall man, younger than Stanley. He was called Jack Turner. I would occasionally glimpse Jack's wife, Kathleen, sitting on a stool in the back room. In front of her on the table would be a pile of bread tins and baking trays, which she would be cleaning. I never saw her out of that room. I think she had a disability. I think I heard it said that Jack wasn't very nice to her. I was about eight and grown-ups were careful what they said in front of me.

I would go to Bonney's for my grandmother, reading from the shopping list she had written. I would cross over the road and push open the glass-fronted door. The old-fashioned shop bell would clang and Mr. Bonney would appear from a back room. He sold a limited amount of groceries as well as bread and cakes. My grandmother would need flour and sugar, which would be weighed out and tipped into two thick blue paper bags. I would also buy margarine, always Echo, a half-pound of butter to mix with the margarine, a packet of biscuits, Brook Bond Dividend Tea and coco powder, plus a loaf of white bread and sometimes as a special treat, warm, sugar covered doughnuts.

The tea would be tightly packed into a packet, no tea bags then. There would be cards in them to collect like cigarette cards. When I returned home, if the tea caddy wasn't empty enough for the new tea to be emptied into it, my grandmother would run a knife along the side of the packet, making a slit just wide enough to be able to get the card out without cutting right through into the tea packet. She would then hand it to me and I always hoped it was a card I hadn't got.

***

These memories were prompted by a family lunch I was cooking one recent Sunday. Earlier in the day I had been down to our local Co-op, just five minutes away. I came home with a basket full of items; vegetables, cooking apples, beer and wine, ice cream, bananas, ice lollies, icing sugar, grapes, oranges and a bottle of Ribena. As I unloaded the shopping, I thought of the basic items my Grandmother used to buy, no impulse daily shopping then, just what was needed and as a rule, one shop a week at Bonney's.

That day, we were having roast pork, a family favourite. Afterwards there will be pork dripping, which older family members will enjoy. I will put the sliced bread into the toaster and whilst waiting for it to pop up, I will think back to when I was a child and I had dripping spread on toast that was made with thick slabs of Bonney's white bread, which I toasted on a long brass toasting fork in front of the fire. The shop closed in 1960.

***

I have my grandmother's recipe book in front of me. It has a faded red cover and is falling to bits and the pages inside are yellowing. My grandmother's writing is on every page and the recipes are written in ink that is fading:

Strawberry whirl
Mary Gibb's fruitcake
Marrow jam
Bright chocolate icing
School cake
Libby's gingerbread
Good luncheon cake

These are some of the recipes and intermingled with the recipes there are cuttings from magazines that have been stuck into the book including:

Something of interest to women
Castor marks on linoleum
Always keep lemons handy as there are so many uses
How to turn pink hydrangeas blue
How to wash bedspreads made of artificial silk taffeta
How to paper a cupboard rather than whitewashing the walls
(this way there was nothing to rub off onto the clean linen)

There was a list of hot puddings for cold days - so now I
know where she got all those steamed pudding recipes from!
I found a fig mould recipe and instructions on how to grow
perfect sweet peas. These were my grandmother's favourite
flower and it conjured up an image of her in her beloved
garden, cutting off the sweet-smelling flowers using her
kitchen scissors with a look of pride on her face as she did so.

***

Sweet Peas

The dusty pathway lay between bracken on one side and a
hawthorn hedge on the other. The May blossom had gone
from the hawthorn branches and now there were the hard,
green haw berries, some starting to turn red. Midsummer's
Day had just passed and the weather had turned to a bright,
blue sky. The dust from the path scuffed up onto the toes of
my sandals and my legs and arms were hot from the sun.

Through a gap in the hedgerow I see an allotment where
potatoes with mauve flowers grow from sandy soil. A breeze
blows a scent in my direction. I recognise it as sweet peas and
see canes covered with the climbing flowers, tumbling in pink,
white, purple, red and the palest of mauve. I move towards the
fence that surrounds the allotment to be near to the flowers
and in doing so I am enveloped by their colour and scent and
I close my eyes to stop the tears from falling. I am a child
again, in the garden with my grandmother. She is cutting
the sweet peas to make a large bunch to take indoors where
they will be placed in a glass vase on the dining room table.
My grandmother is smiling as she does this. I know it is the

flowers that are making her happy.

"Sweet peas are her favourite flowers," Mum had told me.

My grandmother is a First World War widow and the home grown vegetables she harvests are essential to the economy of the family. I did not know that until years later. There is always produce in the garden to bring into the house to eat. In the springtime we sit outside the back door and shell peas. Crisp green pods are snapped open before the small bright green peas are pushed into a colander, always with the warning, "Look out for maggots." The small white larvae play havoc with the crop and every other pod has been chewed to a pulp by the white creatures with their brown heads.

The early potato crop comes into flower. My grandmother takes a fork from the shed and digs deep, turning the earth and bringing the small new potatoes to the surface. "There you are Jane," she would say. "You can pop them into a basket for me."

Taken indoors the potatoes will be scrubbed and put into boiling water with fresh garden mint and a large pinch of salt. The garden mint is also used to make mint sauce, which will be served with Sunday's roast lamb. After washing the mint, the pungent smelling leaves will be stripped from their stalks and my grandmother will place them onto a wooden chopping board and with a large knife, chop into the leaves, pulling them together with the edge of the knife until they were as fine as they could be. The chopped fragments are then put into a jug and stirred together with vinegar and a liberal amount of castor sugar.

Next there is a crop of broad beans, which, whilst in flower, are sprayed with Jeyes fluid to kill the black fly. Rows of small cauliflower plants will be pushed into the earth. This is another hazardous vegetable because when harvested, the thick green caterpillars that live inside the white flower, would somehow manage to hang on to life, even when thoroughly washed and cooked.

Then it is the salad season. There is lettuce. "Be careful to remove the slugs." One always finds its way onto the plate. There are radishes, spring onions, cucumbers and tomatoes. The tomatoes seem to go on for some while with the green ones being used for chutney. Somewhere along the way beetroot is grown. This hard vegetable is often filled with holes from insects. There were carrots too. And carrot fly disease, making more spraying a necessity.

The strawberries are my favourite with a delicious yield of pounds of juicy fruit in the middle of June. When the small white flowers appear, straw is placed around them to lift the strawberries from the earth and provide extra warmth for the ripening of the fruit. As the petals of the flowers fall away, the small green centre grows and ripens into a red strawberry. Sticks and jam pots are arranged to hold aloft a net to shield the fruit from the birds.

At the end of the garden are two plum trees. My grandmother tells me they are called Victorias. The ripe yellow flesh of the purple skinned fruit is often eaten by wasps who then fall drunkenly onto the seared grass. It is the same with the pears that grow high in the branches of the pear tree. As the pears ripen and fall to the ground, the wasps eat into the white flesh of the fruit making the grass appear to move with the crawling insects. My grandmother has her revenge on the wasps. Around the garden and by the back door of the house are jam jars, a mixture of jam and water inside and on top brown paper with holes in. The wasps crawl into the jar and cannot escape. I watch, fascinated, as a jar fills with the yellow and brown insects.

As autumn approaches the garden is tidied and dug over for winter planting. The strawberry net is tied up and hung back in the shed. The canes that held the runner beans are gathered, fastened into bundles and placed alongside the net. Large purple and black beans are saved from the bean pods and placed in a jam jar for next year's crop. The pale green furry pods that formed from the unpicked sweet peas also contain the seed for the following year's flowers. My grandmother empties these tiny brown seeds into jam jars too, ready to plant out when the time is right.

***

At the bottom of the long garden was an apple tree.

"Your grandfather planted that," my mother told me. "It is called a Blenheim Orange."

I went on drawing. My mother was always telling me that. I didn't know what to say. I knew my grandfather had been called Tom and that he had gone away to fight in a war that my mother called the Great War. I knew that he hadn't come back. "It was only a small tree when he planted it," my mother went on. "And now look at it." I was trying to draw a picture of my best friend's cat but I changed it into a tree. I knew that would please my mother.

I liked the garden. When the gooseberries and raspberries were covered in fruit I would go with my best friend Daphne to the bottom of the garden and eat them, sitting in the long grass under the shade of the apple tree. The smell of summer would soak into our limbs. We would break off long stalks of grass and poke at the ants and the small spiders that scuttled in the summer undergrowth.

One morning Daphne called to see me to tell me that she had another sister. "Mum said she wanted a boy, but it is another girl," Daphne said. "I've got four sisters now. This one is called Margaret. She cries a lot." Daphne was allowed to come for tea sometimes, but I didn't often go to her house. Her mother was always too busy with babies.

Autumn came. The grass seared off and a few unpicked hard runner beans flapped on their stalks. The earth was dry and the summer crops were finished for the year. The Blenheim apples that could be reached were gathered with the windfalls picked up off the ground. When my grandmother had cleared the garden of its autumn crops she got the ground ready for leeks, parsnips and celery for Christmas Day. Nothing much happened at Christmas and the time dragged until families became normal again and Daphne would come round. In January long icicles hung from the coal shed roof. Frozen stalks of sprouts stood in the garden alongside white frosted cabbages that my grandmother grew for Sunday lunch.

There was a heavy fall of snow at this time. Daphne and I wore Wellington boots and wrapped up with scarves, coats, gloves and hats. We walked around the garden kicking the stalks of grass that protruded through the snow. Around the bare-leaved gooseberry bushes we built a snowman, sticking an old carrot in its face for a nose and using coal from the shed for its mouth and eyes. In February, the snow melted away and snowdrops pushed through the hard earth and in March, small buds of primroses bloomed in the garden and violets showed under the hedges. Daphne and I played in the black, wooden garden shed where bunches of onions hung and seed-filled jars stood on narrow, uneven shelves. In the corner of the earth-floored shed were a bundle of paper bags containing sweet pea and Sweet William seeds, which my grandmother would plant amongst the vegetables.

April came then. "A treacherous month for gardeners," my grandmother told me.

Daphne's mother was having another baby. "I hope it's a boy," Daphne said. "That's what Mum and Dad want."

Green shoots were pushing through brown earth then. The wind was warmer and a pale sun shone through the clouds. I sat by the window drawing, waiting for Daphne to come. My mother came into the room, "Look at the blossom on the trees," she said. "And look at that apple tree. Your grandfather planted that before he went to war. It's called a Blenheim Orange. Lovely, isn't it?"

Chapter Eight

My grandmother lived her life with a routine, as people did back then. She appeared to be a very contented person. In later years she had a bad heart and was advised not to walk up hills, not easy as our house was at the top of a hill. She had a tot of whisky every morning – for medicinal purposes of course. She enjoyed the garden, cooking and playing the card game of cribbage. On these occasions my grandmother would have friends to visit her and the fire in the front room would be lit. A green baize covered square card table would be put up. The legs of the table would be folded out and clicked into place and four chairs placed around it. My grandmother would fetch a pack of cards and a long board with holes in. I would watch as the four ladies laid the cards in turn and would hear them say, "Fifteen two, fifteen four and two is six," or someone would cut the cards and it would be, "one for his knob" or "two for his heels." I would watch as the ladies counted the holes before putting the small pegs into the holes. I was told that the game was called cribbage.

My grandmother enjoyed horse racing and placing a small bet, and television when we got one in later years. Ours was rented from a local shop and even the afternoon rests did not take place if there was a horse race on, especially if Edward

Hyde was the jockey. She took the Sunday newspaper, the News of the World, to study the form of the horses and to read about Eddie Hyde. She made her bets at Eddie King's. He was the local watchmaker and ran a book, which wasn't legal in those days.

Whist drives were popular then. My grandmother would go and there would be a snowball – an extra prize, which started as a small amount and would mount up each week until it was won. It was pointed out to me that winning that would make a difference to my grandmother's income.

I can see my grandmother dressed in her grey suit with a walking stick, going to the hall at the end of our road for a bus outing for the over 70s club. I am 74 and cannot imagine going to an over 70's club; how times change. In her early 70s my grandmother had a slight stroke and because of this, the organizer Mrs. Harvey told her that she could not go on an outing to Felixstowe. My grandmother turned around walked home and never attempted to go on another outing. My mother related the story to me and told me how upset my grandmother had been.

Two streets away was the Bias Binding Factory from where my grandmother would collect boxes which contained small pieces of card, bundles of small cellophane bags, elastic bands, labels and large reels of coloured binding. She made a circular cork mat through which she put a large nail. She would place one of the reels onto the nail and picking up a card she would begin to wind the coloured binding onto it. I would count the twists; five twists, or was it six, on each of the four rows and then the end would be tucked under one of the rows with a pair of scissors. A label would be put around the card and the card would be slipped into one of the narrow cellophane bags. The end flap would then be wetted and stuck down. My grandmother kept a small damp orange sponge in a small blue bowl for this. When a roll of the binding was finished, the cards would counted out into dozens and an elastic band would be put around these. When all the reels of binding were finished my grandmother would return the box to the factory. Her work would be inspected and she would be paid accordingly and then return home with another box of binding. My grandmother was known as an outworker. Sitting in the firelight on a winter's evening in a wicker chair, I would watch my grandmother as she wound the coloured fabric round the narrow cards. Then I would help her count them into dozens before putting them into the box.

My aunt, Dah lived at home until she married, at the age of 45, a local widower called Sam Bloomfield. Sam owned a garage in Framlingham and drove a black car with worn leather seats that was used for a taxi. We didn't own a car so going out in his car was an occasion. I would sit on a small, folding canvas seat with my back against the door so I looked out of the side window on the opposite side of the car. Watching the countryside from that angle made me feel sick and Sam drove at 20mph or less which didn't help. To help my nausea, a metal chain was tied to the back bumper of the car. As the chain trailed along the road it was supposed to counteract something that caused the sickness. I was also told to hold a penny coin in my hand as that would help. But neither idea worked. I always had to behave, not that I was naughty, but my aunt would say this as she was disapproving of me. Maybe these outings were a nuisance to her? To me,

Dah always seemed cross and I was apprehensive of her, even when she was dying with stomach cancer. My husband and I nursed her at our home until she died, but I felt like a small child always waiting to be told off. It didn't seem natural to be caring for her and to see her in such a vulnerable state.

On the beach trips, we would go to Thorpeness and other places, but the journeys spoilt these outings. I felt a tension from Uncle Sam. It was as if he would rather have been doing something else. Once again, I was mindful of my behavior. Uncle Sam came from a different era when children should be seen and not heard.

By looking at old pictures I know that on some occasions my grandmother would come to the beach with us. She had a walking stick by this time and it is amazing to think she was probably the same age as I am now.

My cousin, Pip, daughter of my mother's brother Bill has her own memories of our grandmother, which she wrote to me in a letter:

July, 2009

"Dear Jane,

Finally I have managed to get some memories down on paper. It seems like very little when I think that Nanny was a major figure in the first three years of my life. Also, that we were together for seven or eight weeks every summer. Filey Convent (where we went to school) always had eight weeks off for summer and as far as I can remember we spent all, or certainly most of them, in Fram with you all.

Another memory that I forgot to mention – Nanny's flower

garden, always glorious and the big garden filled with fruit and vegetables. In the war Nanny used to take cut flowers to the Crown Hotel and fill the vases there. That is where she met the young American Air Force men and invited them over for Sunday lunch and Bill Kloeblen was one of them.

Tall, rather forbidding, a warm smile and grey hair, usually up in a bun, but at night in a long plait down her back. I used to get into bed with Nanny in the mornings and we would play a fantasy game. We would drive around Fram starting at the top of the Freehold and we would 'pick up' all the children en route to go on a trip together. First Pamela Bullingham, then down the Freehold on the right to get Gillian Coates, up through the village to get Diana Norman and then to the Freeman's shop to get Anthea and her sister Hilary. I can't remember anyone else or where we used to go on our fantasy trip, but we played this game very often.

Nanny made the greatest rabbit pies and baked hobney-dobs, which were little pastry lumps joined together with pink or white icing (these were my favourites). She also made chocolate buns, which Anne loved, but I found them too dry. I once made strawberry jam with Nanny, but she kept getting stung on her fingers by wasps and I didn't fancy getting stung so kept my distance and didn't stay long. Nanny taught me to make scrambled eggs also.

During the war – this means up until May 1944 – we used to have to get up at night and go downstairs under the huge metal table whenever there were air raids. There were wire sides on the table, which were slotted into place once we were all in. Nanny used to make everyone nervous by getting up to peel carrots for me to eat – I still love raw carrots.

I used to go with Nanny to the big shed where the mangle stood – she always told me to keep my fingers out of the way when she mangled the clothes to get the water out.

Once we moved up to Hull, we used to always go to Fram on the train for our summer holidays. We always arrived about teatime and Nanny welcomed us with a high tea of self-boiled ham, salad (from the big garden) brown bread and a big plate of cakes.

My mother told me she was very in awe of her mother-in-law. However once, when Nanny came to stay with her and asked what she could do to help, mother asked her to do the dusting. Afterwards my mother noticed that Nanny had only dusted around the ornaments and not lifted them up – this made mother realise that Nanny was human after all and in future she did not hold her in quite so much awe!

Once during our summer holidays when I was about nine or 10, Anne six or seven and Jane five or six we all went out for a meal in a café in Ipswich – this was a very rare event and we three girls were very excited. Nanny (sat) at the head of the table and when things were getting too loud she stood up and said in an exasperated tone, "You children are being much too loud, you need to behave yourselves." So saying she made a sharp downward hand movement with her arm, her hand caught her glass of Guinness and the beer flooded down the length of the table! Mother and Mary tried to stifle their laughter and we three children were horrified! Mother told me this story many times over the years and she always giggled.

When we all went off to Thorpeness for the day Nanny never came with us. She helped make sandwiches, packed them up into big square biscuit tins along with buns and cake, but she then waved us off at the door. At the time I could not understand why she would want to forgo the trip to the seaside, but in retrospect I imagine she was only too happy to have a respite from the three cousins!

Nanny always had a rest after lunch and we were not allowed to be noisy or play the piano during this time. (The piano) was in the front room directly below Nanny's bedroom. Nanny loved card games and she taught me to play cribbage. She also loved to play bowls. She was a great knitter and she knitted Fair Isle jumpers and berets. I also remember her knitting socks using four needles. She once sewed me a little grey Piglet, as in Winnie-the-Pooh. I remember she covered one of those old-fashioned cloth buttons (which had two eyelets within metal) with the grey piglet material for his nose.

On the day we left Fram in a hire car with Pat to move to Yorkshire, Nanny cooked me a delicious, big fried breakfast – however driving in the car did not agree with me and we kept having to stop for me to sick. Nanny was a much better cook than my Irish grandmother in Hull and I always looked forward to her delicious food in the summer!"

Chapter Nine

The Three Graces

Kate Crane born November 6, 1880
Ada Crane born February 3, 1882 (my grandmother)
Alice Crane born January 1886

Kate, Ada and Alice were sisters, born in the later part of the
19th century. As they grew and blossomed into young women
they became known as the Three Graces. I know nothing
about their childhood or the childhood of any of the family,
except that they lived in Gold Street, Northampton and were
quite well to do.

When I knew my aunts, Kitty and Alice, they lived at 12,
Woodland Avenue in the town they were born in. When I
visited them as a child, their house seemed large and dark
with a brown wooden banister, stairs and brown carpets. The
kitchen had cream walls and cupboards painted green. The
aunts had a lady called Mrs. Howe who came in five days a
week to clean and cook. If she was there when I visited she
would call me, "my duck" and give me a glass of weak orange
juice and a dry rich tea biscuit. In the sitting room there was
a large aspidistra and a leather chaise lounge on which Auntie

Kitty would be laying with a small brown bottle in her hand that contained smelling salts. She always wore a long, pale green, woollen dress and long, dangling earrings of a thin gold chain with a piece of turquoise stone on the end. In the pictures of her youth she was a beautiful looking woman with thick hair that was piled and pinned on top of her head. Auntie Kitty was my favourite as she talked the most and had, what I would now call, charisma.

When I look at pictures of Auntie Alice, she seems the more thoughtful one. Her eyes seem sad and wistful, but perhaps that is my imagination. I discovered on the census that both Kit and Alice were schoolteachers up until the time they retired, but I know little about that. They didn't work when I knew them.

Auntie Alice was quiet, almost subservient to Kitty whom she waited on hand and foot, referring back to her about everything that was to be done. After Auntie Kitty died, Auntie Alice became depressed and went in and out of hospital before coming to live with my mother. By this time, I was married and my grandmother, Alice's sister, had died.

Auntie Alice's once lovely hair was grey and fine and there were always a large number of hairpins escaping from the bun she tried to style. She didn't like the sun. In the summer she wore a large straw hat with a brown ribbon around the top of the brim. My Mum, who was kind but didn't always think things through, couldn't cope, so Auntie Alice had to go into a home in Bungay which was quite a way from Framlingham. When she became physically ill she went into Norwich hospital where she died. There was a real to-do when my mother inherited money from the aunt's estate, which came from the sale of the house. Her cousins wrote dreadful letters to her accusing her of looking after Aunt Alice just for money. The cousins hadn't done anything to help with either Kitty or Alice in their later years and these cousins were all married with husbands, whereas my mother didn't have anyone to provide for her.

When I look at the second of the Three Graces, my grandmother, I think that maybe she was the least attractive of the three. However, she was the only one that married. Despite being widowed and left with three young children to bring up I think my grandmother had the best of lives married to a man who loved her and with whom she had three children. She had tenacity and a spirit to her that her sisters lacked.

Looking back, I can see that Auntie Kitty was a self-centred woman who sucked the life out of her sister Alice. That's just how it was I suppose, through upbringing and circumstances. They were both careful with money. My mother told me that they never ate a whole tomato but instead had one between them.

Years later I visited Northampton and went to the house in Woodland Avenue where my two great aunts lived. Whilst I stood outside a lady came out, curious to see what I was doing. I explained and she asked me in to look around. The house seemed so small. In the dining room where the bookcases, china ornaments and the polished table covered with a red chenille cloth had been, there were children's toys, books and bright wall paper. The French windows opened into the garden, again much smaller than I remembered. Where there had been a birdbath and neat beds of aubrietia and pink phlox, there was now a swing and paddling pool and a sand pit.

***

When I was a child, I saw a cuckoo in a nest. My two great aunts, Alice and Kitty, had been visiting. They had white, thin, papery skin and wrinkles and had been old for as long as I could remember. Years later I saw Auntie Alice lying in a bed in a Norwich hospital, frail hands clutching at the sheets, grey hair tangled around her head, her night dress unbuttoned, showing a shrivelled sagging breast. Auntie Kitty had died before her sister. She had made my mother promise to prick her arm with a pin to make sure that the blood did not run, which would prove that she was really dead. Auntie Kitty had lived her life in fear of being buried alive.

I don't remember my great aunts coming to stay very often. They lived in Northampton and hired a car and driver when they wanted to come to visit. Auntie Kitty hated draughts and wouldn't have the car windows open, even though Auntie Alice used to sit in the back of the car feeling sick. My mother thought Auntie Kitty was selfish to order her sister about the way she did, but my grandmother said it was Alice's fault for letting her.

Auntie Kitty was tall and slim. She had thick, brown hair, which she wore piled onto the top of her head and pinned in place with large hairpins. She always wore a long skirt and a blouse with ruffles down the front and a high collar with a gold pin at the neck. On special occasions she wore turquoise drop earrings. I thought she was the more interesting of the two sisters. I found Auntie Alice rather dull by comparison.

When the aunts stayed in Suffolk they used to take afternoon walks over the fields at the back of the house. The fields were called Moore's Meadows after the farmers they had once belonged too. The fields are now a housing estate, but when I was a child it was a wonderful place to explore, with tadpoles and small fish in the stream and long green grass on the banks and shady oak trees to picnic under.

It was on a walk over these meadows that I saw a cuckoo. The aunts were staying and I had gone for a walk with them. We crossed the small bridge over the stream onto the top meadow. I could see the thick jelly of frogspawn in the still deep part of the water and on the bank were clusters of primroses. Ahead of us were clumps of thick hawthorn bushes. Auntie Kitty walked in front of us. "I love bird nesting," she called back to us. She was out of sight when Auntie Alice and I heard her shout, "Look," she said, "I've found a cuckoo on a nest."

I ran towards her and Auntie Kitty lifted me up to show me the nest, poking her thin-gloved finger into the wide-open, orange mouth of the bird, laughing as she did so. "Ooh, it nearly had my finger off. It's a good job I had gloves on." She shook her hand and laughed again. I could smell the mothballs that the aunts kept amongst their clothes. Putting me down on the grass Auntie Kitty said, "Just fancy, it's the first time I have seen a cuckoo. It has just taken over that nest and pushed the eggs or the other fledglings out. That's what cuckoos do. They don't build their own nests." She turned and called to her sister. "Do come and look Alice and get a move on dear."

Auntie Alice leaned over and peered into the hedge. "Yes, it's very nice dear. But don't you think we should be getting back? It's getting chilly."

Auntie Alice's brown hat had fallen to one side. She pushed it straight, securing it with her pearl hatpin. Auntie Kitty's eyes sparkled as she looked at the bird. "The female cuckoo just lays the egg and bob's your uncle," she said. "Someone else does all the work." I listened to the conversation. I remembered my mother saying that Auntie Alice did all the work for Auntie Kitty.

I walked with my aunts down the slope of the green meadow. We climbed over the small stile and out onto the road that led back to the house. The aunts both wore a fox fur around their necks. I watched the dangling heads of the fox, their glass eyes shining, their mouths lined with thick strips of black that clipped onto the lackluster tails.

The aunts returned to their home in Northampton with Auntie Kitty sitting in the front of the car surrounded by blankets and closed windows. Auntie Alice sat in the back, feeling sick, and surrounded by luggage. I waved them off and forgot about the cuckoo.

I was in my early 20s when the two aunts died. Auntie Kitty went first, followed 18 months later by her sister Alice. Their Edwardian house, number 12 Woodland Avenue, was sold. I helped my mother sort out the contents of the house. It was early summer and when we had finished I went out into the garden. It was evening, and the light was fading. The heavy summer air was scented with the smell of rain and leaves. I heard the faint echoing sound of the cuckoo with its solitary song that heralded summer and for a moment I became a small child again remembering the shrill, excited laughter of Auntie Kitty on those green meadows where rows of houses now stand.

**

Chapter Ten

La Plume Est Sur La Table
(The Pen Is On the Table)

The part of this story where I appear is true. The rest is as it might have been ...

1906

"Ada, look over here. What do you think of this one? It's oak, a nice wood."

Sunlight reflected through the small shop window onto the polished tabletop. Ada looked at it and ran her hands over the grained wood. "It's nice Tom and the chairs are strong and high backed." She sat down on one of them. "They're comfortable too."

"The label says two guineas, Ada, and that includes the chairs. We've got enough money. What do you think?"

Ada nodded at him and Tom squeezed her hand. "We'll take them then," he said.

Ada smiled. "They'll look lovely in our dining room and there's plenty of room for the baby when he is big enough to sit with us."

"Yes," Tom winked at her, "and there's four places, so room

for another one."

Ada's face flushed, but she smiled at Tom before looking away and back to the table.

1912

Ada carried the turkey through into the dining room and laid the large plate carefully on the table.

"That looks good enough to eat," Tom said. "Look what your Mum has cooked, Mary." He moved the red crackers to one side and pulled the dish towards him, smiling at his wife as he did so. "You're a marvellous cook, love," he said. And then to the baby on his lap he said, "You're too young Billy to know what I am saying, but your Mum's a grand cook." He handed Billy to his wife and stood up, sharpening the knife, before carving the perfectly cooked meat.

1915

The curtains were drawn over the window. The room was quiet except for the ticking of the clock. Ada sat reading and re-reading the telegram that she held in her hand: Missing, believed killed.

She laid the telegram on the table, smoothing the thin yellow paper over with her fingers, running her thumb under the name. Tom Nicholls …missing …believed killed. In her head she could hear the brass band playing as Tom had marched off …

"I'll be back love," he promised. "Look after the children and take care. I've got a lovely family Ada. You don't think I wouldn't come back to you do you?" He kissed her, squeezing her shoulder as he turned to leave.

1918

Ada walked the short distance to the end of the road to meet the postman, which she did every morning. The telegram had said, missing, believed killed. As no confirmation had come she hoped, as she did each day, for news that he had been found alive. She hoped that he had just lost his memory and would return to her. She had stopped crying months ago. There were the children to bring up and a life to get on with.

The familiar bike stood against the wall. The postman knew what she was waiting for. There were many women that met him each morning. "Sorry Mrs. Nicholls," he said, "nothing for you today."

"Thank you," Ada said and turned and walked back to her house, feeling as she entered it, the sadness that had been with her since the telegram had arrived. The war had been over for just over one year and still there had been no positive confirmation about her husband.

Going through into the dining room she set the table for breakfast.

1944

"Mary, quick, get up. The sirens have gone off again. Downstairs, hurry girl."

Mary, still half asleep, heard her mother's anxious voice. She stood, sleepily wrapping her dressing gown around her swollen body. Oh god, she thought, only two weeks to go until the baby is born. What would happen if it came tonight?

In her hurry she stumbled on the stairs and steadied herself by holding onto the stair rail. In the dining room she pushed herself under the table with her mother Ada squeezing in

beside her and placing the pieces of corrugated tin against
the sides of the table for protection. Overhead she heard the
planes. I'm so frightened, she thought. She felt her mother's
hand in hers. There was a whine overhead, the house shook,
and then silence. Scrambling out from under the table she and
her mother opened the door of their house and looked down
the street. At the end of the short road there was smoke where
a house had stood.

1950

"What a lovely tea your Mum has done Jane; even with
rationing there's a good spread. Six today, what a big girl you're
getting."

On the table were egg and cress sandwiches piled high on blue
and white plates, bowls of red and green jelly and small, pink
iced buns. Standing in the centre was a cake with pink icing and
six candles on, with the words Happy Birthday Jane iced onto it.
She felt hot under her blue velvet dress and the collar poked into
her neck. Her friends sat in their places with their names written
on small pieces of white card and laid on their plates.

"Shall we sing?" said her mother as she lit the candles on
the cake. "Happy birthday to you, happy birthday dear Jane,
happy birthday to you."

Jane felt her face go red. Taking a big breath, she blew out
five of the six candles on the cake.

"Oh, what a shame," her mother said, "you won't get your
wish now. Still you can wish anyway. It might still work."

After the food was eaten, games were played; musical chairs,
pass the parcel, spin the plate and blind man's bluff. Jane wasn't
good at games. She always felt so conspicuous.

1951

"Can I get down now Nannie?" Jane asked.

"Yes, dear," her grandmother replied.

"Thank you for the tea," Jane said, as she pushed the plate away.

Her grandmother loaded up the dirty crockery onto a tray and carried it through into the kitchen, returning with a tin of polish and a duster. Jane's Mum Mary came through into the room. "You and that table, mother," she said. "You'll polish it away."

1952

"Put the top back on the chocolate spread, Jane. Have you had enough to eat dear?"

"Yes, thank you," Jane told her mother. She felt her legs itching under the long, woollen socks she wore. "Can I wear short socks, Mum?" she pleaded. "It's so hot and my legs itch."

"It's not the end of May yet," her mother replied. "You know the saying about not casting a clout until May is out."

I should do, Jane thought, I've heard it enough times. She rubbed the top of her legs against the cool curved wood of the table legs.

"Elbows off the table dear." Jane's grandmother came into the room. "When I was young I had a wooden yard stick put behind my back and slipped through the loop of my arms, so I had to sit up straight." Her grandmother proudly pulled back her shoulders. "That's why my back is so straight." She smiled as she looked at her granddaughter. What a pity Tom wasn't here to see her. Such a sadness that he had been killed in the war all those years ago.

1956

Jane ran the pen nib along a dark brown grain in the table and watched as the ink made a black line in the wood. The fire in the grate crackled and small bright sparks hung on the sooty chimney bricks. Warm steam rose from the ironed clothes that were airing on the wooden horse from the heat of the fire. She continued with her homework. The nib of the pen was clogged up and she gave it two hard shakes. Four blots of ink spattered onto the pale brown and pink flowered wallpaper beside her. At that moment her mother came through from the kitchen, her eyes going straight away to the ink marks on the wallpaper.

"Oh Jane, what will Nannie say! She saved for months to get this room decorated and it has only just been done!"

"I didn't mean to do it. I just shook the pen, that's all." Jane's eyes returned to the ink stains, which having soaked into the paper were now bigger than at first.

"No, I don't suppose you did," her mother sighed, "but you can tell Nannie about it. I hope you have nearly finished your homework."

"Just about."

Her mother moved the clotheshorse away from the fire, lifted the brown kettle that stood on the blue tiles of the fireplace and pushed it onto the hot coals. Jane heard a hissing noise as water slopped out of the spout onto the flames. Her mother's voice interrupted her thoughts. "I wish you were learning French, Jane. I did it at the Grammar School when I was a child. I wasn't very good though. All I can remember is 'la plume is on la tableau', the pen is on the table." She smiled, "I wonder what French is for 'the ink is on the wall'. Come on. Let's clear the table. It's just about tea time and the kettle will boil any minute."

1964

The table had been extended to put the coffin on. Her grandmother, Ada, lay shrouded in pink with her arms crossed and folded across her chest. Her eyes were closed, her face peaceful. Jane leant forward and kissed the white forehead. She hadn't realised that it would feel so cold and hard. "Goodbye Nannie," she said.

She had never seen anyone dead before. It was strange how small her grandmother seemed now and so shrunken. It was almost as though there wasn't a body there, but just the head and a long, pale pink, satin dress.

1974

"Come on Sarah and Selena, it's teatime." Jane stood calling them from the kitchen window. "Give your father a shout too please." Minutes later the two girls rushed in. "Where have you two been? No, don't tell me. Wash your hands ready for tea and make sure you remove all the dirt."

Jane had laid blue tea plates on the white cloth on which stood large plates of brown bread, ham, chocolate cake, strawberries and cream. She stood admiring her Sunday tea. It did look lovely. Four high backed chairs stood around the square table with a white cloth covering the marks on the oak wood. Her husband John came into the room, his large frame blocking out the light as he stood in the doorway. "That looks nice," he said. He kissed his wife's cheek and she grinned at him.

"Thanks," she said. "Glad I'm appreciated." She poured the tea out and watched as her family helped themselves to food.

1976

Sarah and Selena had hung rugs around the table. "Look Mum," Sarah pulled at her mother's hand, "look at our camp." Jane bent down. "Come on Mum, come in with us."

Jane crawled under the table, smelling the mustiness of the grey blanket as it brushed against her face. Light filtered in through thin holes in the blanket.

"Mind, that's the lookout space. Great isn't it?" Selena said.

"It's great," she said, "now would you like some tea? Your Nan will be here soon." Jane thought about her mother who had not had the happiest of lives, but she loved the grandchildren and enjoyed being with them.

1984

The day was hot and the French windows were open. Jane glanced down at the oak table. One day she would get it resurfaced or maybe even get a new one. A soft breeze blew in, ruffling the petals of the pansies that stood in a blue bowl on the table. Pansies for thoughts, Jane thought. She picked up her pen wondering what to write: Mary, beloved mother of Jane, she began. She moved her hand away from the paper and ran the nib along the deep black ink groove in the oak wood. Her mother's voice echoed in her head, "la plume is on la tableau."

She continued to write, peacefully at home, Mary, beloved mother of Jane and daughter of Ada and Thomas Nicholls.

Chapter Eleven

My grandmother died at home on September 4, 1965. One evening she looked into the distance, beyond the foot of the bed and said, "It's all right. They've come to meet me. Bert and Tom. I am so very tired. Nothing matters anymore."

The dining room had been turned into a bedroom and her bed was in the corner under the window. I took my eleven-month-old daughter, Sarah, to see her. My grandmother took her hand and said, "What a lovely a baby." A few days later I was in the kitchen with my mother and aunt and a silence fell. I realised my grandmother's rattling breath had stopped.

My Nan was a great one for sayings. In my autograph book she wrote, "Do your best and leave the rest, 'twill all come right some day or night." I do hope it did come right for her and I do hope that Tom and Bert, her brother, were there to meet her.

***

I was just a child in the shadows always aware that there were three people to please and not to upset. When Sarah was born, I was young and busy. Now it is too late to ask my grandmother any questions, but the spirit and essence of my grandmother lives on through me I feel, with my practical nature and through my cooking.

***

After my grandmother died, my mother continued to live at number 13, Albert Road until her death in 1984. In 1962 my mother bought the house. She had been in hospital when the owner put them up for auction and her neighbor, Mr. Watts, bought the pair for £700. My mother told Mr. Watts that she wished she had known as she would have liked to have bought her side of the two houses. He said that as she was a good neighbor he would let her buy number 13 for £700, the price he paid for the pair of them.

My aunt, Dah, came to see my mother each afternoon. By this time her husband Sam had died. They used to play scrabble, but I think they irritated each other. Before that Dah would visit most mornings to see her mother.

My mother's health deteriorated over the years and she suffered constant illnesses. She continued to live in the same house for the rest of her life. Like my grandmother, my mother rarely spoke much of the past, just sometimes mentioning her brother and the May Balls she had gone to when her brother was at Cambridge.

When my mother died, not at home but after six week in a narrow, isolated hospital bed, I sold the house, emptying it of 70 years of being lived in by the same family. I got rid of old pieces of furniture that were worn out, but I kept the square oak dining room table and chairs that had been my grandmother's, as they were my favourite pieces. I also kept the large chest of drawers that had been in my aunt's bedroom, a small writing desk and a few ornaments including pieces of Poole pottery, two pretty paper weights, which I have on my kitchen window sill, and a small brass bell in the shape of lady with a long skirt on. This had been given to my mother by her brother.

A schoolteacher and his wife bought the house. They began to alter it, but then they moved because of a promotion they were both offered. They rented the house out to an American family, The Garcias, in 1988. I got to know them when the middle child, Elaine, aged four, knocked on our door and asked if she could play in my house. It was when my first husband, John, was alive. Elaine took to him. I wrote a story based on this called A Knock at the Door.

When I first got to know the Garcias, they would ask me down for a drink. I noticed there was still the same flooring in the dining room that had been there when my mother was alive. The kitchen had been altered with pine units installed. There was a wood burner in the front room. As I walked into the house, I felt myself shiver and the long hall passage seemed as daunting as ever. The house also had a pleasant smell that I associate with Americans and some parcels I received as a child from relatives of my grandmother. I knew nothing about these relatives but they sent me clothes a couple of times a year, and occasionally food. I also caught a faint smell of mustiness that had always been there.

The Garcias went back to America in the early 1990s. Trena, the eldest daughter was 12 and now she is 40. Divorced, remarried, an army nurse, she served in Afghanistan, leaving her children in the care of friends, and has now retired from the army. She stays in touch and came to see me once with her two young children. She brought me a silver Pandora bracelet. "You will never know what you meant to me," she said. It was 1.30 in the morning. She had just arrived from Heathrow in a taxi with her children, who she put straight upstairs to bed. Trena has moved on. I have stayed in the same place. Now, once again, the house is up for sale. To see the house when I walk up the road I have to look to the right. I rarely do it. It is just a house I lived in a long time ago.

After the Garcias, the house was sold again to another schoolteacher who was married with three young children. I chatted to them, told them I was born there and they asked me in. They had altered the house completely. The small front bedroom had become a bathroom and the downstairs bathroom had been turned into a utility room. The step-down back bedroom had become a brightly coloured nursery and my grandmother's old room was now decorated in various shades of dusky pink. A large pine bed was covered with a brightly coloured duvet and faced a different direction from my grandmother's bed. They gave me a tour and I had stood, looking at the bed, then turning away embarrassed at the sharp image of Sharon, curled up with her school teacher husband.

There were clothes thrown on the floor and books on pine shelving that lined the walls. There was a small television in the corner of the room. It was all different, yet the room had a familiarity about it. I felt a coldness run through my body, a feeling that my mother used to describe as, "if someone had walked over my grave".

Central heating had been installed. The hall, now warm, was painted in soft grey with white wainscoting. The brown staircase and hallway were carpeted in a matching pale grey carpet and the stair railings were painted white. A large round white paper shade covered the hall light bulb and a mobile of white glass doves hung above the staircase. The dining room was painted in Wedgwood blue and the cupboards that had been on either side of the fireplace had been removed to make way for pine shelving and soft lighting. On the floor was a pale blue carpet and pretty blue-flowered curtains hung at the window.

Looking out into the garden, I saw that the coal shed that had stood against the dividing wall had gone and that the back yard had become a paved patio area. In place of the straggly privet hedge that had surrounded the garden there was a high wooden fence on which trailed honeysuckle and clematis. At the end of the garden was a carport.

"We love the house," Sharon told me. "It has such a lovely feel to it."

"Do you?" I gave a small shrug. "I'm afraid I never liked it."

"Not even now it's changed?" Sharon's expression was anxious, eager to please.

Sharon's husband got the offer of another job and like previous residents, they moved on. A young lady bought the old house. The postman told me her name was Ursula.

Passing by the house one day, I noticed new white and blue flowered curtains draping the window. I could see a round table on which stood a bowl of bright yellow daffodils and a framed picture standing in the bay window. Ursula hadn't been moved in long. Around the corner of the house laid a pile of cardboard. I knocked on the door using the same black knocker that had been there when I was a child, to see if I could have the cardboard for a friend who collected it to sell, using the proceeds for charity. Ursula seemed surprised but said it was okay. She expressed her irritation at the parking on the road. "Well, it is a private road," I explained to her, "and very much a give and take road when to comes to parking." Then I added. "I live on this road," and pointed to the front bedroom. "I was born in this house in that room," I said.

Her voice softened then. "Oh," she said. "Do come in and have a look around. I didn't like the pine and I have started doing some alterations, but I have a lot more to do."

I hesitated, but I didn't go in. "I haven't got time at the moment," I said.

"Oh well, perhaps when it is all finished you'd like to see it?"

"Thank you," I said and walked away. I didn't want to look around the house. I knew the view from the window would still be the same.

***

I have always been aware of the atmosphere in houses or anywhere, probably due to my childhood. I never minded being an only child and I never hankered or even thought what it would be like to have siblings, even in later life. In fact, it seems when I hear of family disagreements between brothers and sisters, that being an only child makes life a lot easier. However, I have always felt sad about not having a father who cared for me. It would have been lovely to have had a kind Dad. I do feel I missed out on that. My childhood was not unhappy. It was what it was and it helped me to be the person I have become. I know there wasn't any real fun, except when my two cousins came. To this day I am not good at fun. I do however have a good sense of humour, which I hope shows in my writing. I was an anxious child, aware of the tensions in the house, which I didn't know or understand at the time. My aunt, who I think was bitter about life, must have been happy once. I see that in some of the photographs of her taken at Thorpeness with her brother and my mother. I didn't know much about her early life but I think there was someone she had been keen on. Maybe she would have liked children. The word that sums her up is disapproving, always disapproving.

My mother, suffering from the shame of divorce, not in the best of health, put all her attention onto me. She was not a tough lady, unlike her mother. I was her entire life and it was not easy for her when I left to get married, although I saw her most days.

When my grandmother died, she left £200 to my mother and £100 to Dah. This was because my aunt had a husband, a house and an income and my mother didn't. My aunt was upset about this so thinking about it, I imagine she was jealous of my mother. My mother used the money to buy a red and cream Hillman Minx and took to the road. She could be a bit scary in that car. She had got her license during the war when no test was required. She drove down to Devon and missed seeing my father by a whisker. When she went around a roundabout, she stuck her arm out of the window, but it was more of a wave than a signal.

***

My mother's second husband John Stainbank, who took his own life in July, 1972, owned number 14, Albert Road, which is how I came to move back onto Albert Road with my husband, John, and my daughters Sarah and Selena in 1974. Our son, JB, was born in 1977. I have lived on this P-shaped road, which has 19 houses, for 64 years of my 74 years.

***

My friend Heather who lived on Albert Road, and who I am still in touch with, wrote to me to say, "I think every now and then of the old days in Framlingham. Remembering this, I do recollect how Mrs. Nicholls's veggie garden was unlike other people's inasmuch that children were not allowed to rampage around. Veggie patches were usually the domain of men and there were a few thistles and old overgrown bushes in hers. I know her two apple trees were special. Perhaps they were planted by her husband".

Chapter Twelve

Returning to 13 Albert Road, Framlingham

An imagining of what might have happened if I had gone away and returned.

I had always known that I would return to the house one day. It hadn't seemed important to me when I had left it, but now, all these years later, I knew that I had to go back. I had seen the house advertised in an estate agents leaflet that I had picked up in London. It read, "desirable semi-detached residence, ideal weekend retreat or family home. Three beds, fitted bathroom, sitting room, pine kitchen and central heating throughout. Pleasant enclosed garden. Must be viewed to be appreciated." Details followed about the market town I knew so well. I was puzzled about the small, enclosed garden. It had been a large garden in my childhood. Also there had been four bedrooms. I phoned the estate agent and made an appointment for the following day. I was instructed to collect the key from the local agent. "What is madam looking for?" I was asked. I told the man I wasn't sure. I didn't tell him that I was just l wanted to look at the house.

I left London early. The day was clear and bright. The

journey was easy and soon I had left London behind. I stopped on the way at a Little Chef restaurant, not liking the brick eating houses that had sprung up in the English countryside. I ate hot rolls washed down with strong black coffee. I thought of the house I was going back to and the market town that I had not visited for 25 years. I finished my coffee and continued my drive.

When I had left the house it was a post-war, freezing cold, undesirable residence without a bathroom or an inside lavatory. I thought of the hot summer days in the garden when as a child, I had picked the ripe red strawberries that my grandmother had grown and had sat eating them with the juice running down my chin. I remembered the hard gooseberries that dried my mouth with their sourness as I bit into them and the pink sticks of rhubarb that I had dipped into sugar before I crunched the soft yellow flesh. I had made rose petal scent, pushing the fallen rose petals into a jam jar before covering the petals with water. I had dug in the brown earth for small pieces of blue china. I wondered why people had buried their broken china in the earth, but I hadn't wondered that as a child. Again, I remembered the heat as I had laid under the apple tree and smelt the sun on my skin.

In my mind I went from the garden into the small, brick-floored kitchen and the back place, a small room where the brooms, polishes, bags of saved string and paper bags were kept.

The lavatory had been in the garden at the end of the concrete yard. Large black spiders had lived there. When the autumn nights got colder they would come into the house. On dark nights I would go to the lavatory holding a candle for light, hoping that no one would be lurking in the darkness to pounce out at me. I would nearly burst on a winter's evening rather than go outside.

My memory took me back indoors again. I thought of the long corridor that had been full of shadows leading to the brown painted door that opened to the draughty front room. This room was out of bounds, except for special days including Christmas when the room would smell of pine needles from the Christmas tree and the purple baubles that hung from its branches would reflect the firelight. I thought of the paper chains that were got out year after year and the pork dripping spread on toast that was toasted on a special fork by the fire. It was in this room that I had entertained my first boyfriend. My mother had never come into that room when David was there.

"He is such a nice boy," my mother had said. I wonder what she would have said if she had walked in on us?

The heart of the house had been the small dining room. It was the room most used. In the winter and cold days there would be a flickering fire there. The butter would be softening in the hearth in a small Pyrex dish and a kettle of water would be on the fire. On the floor there was dark red and blue linoleum that I had to polish every Saturday morning. I remembered the dark brown paint on the door, windowsills and skirting board, the brown and pink wallpaper and brown curtains.

I shivered. Now I was driving into the small town. It had changed. There were more houses, but it was recognisable, like someone growing old, looking the same but different. I collected the key from the agents and leaving my car parked on the market square I walked to my childhood home. The paint on the front door and windowsills was green now, but the jasmine bush, which had always been there, still grew against the wall. I stood, hesitating, wondering what I would find. The front door, now painted green and white, still had the same large cast iron door knocker on it. I couldn't resist banging it against the door. The sound would have vibrated through the house. I half expected my grandmother to answer the door. Turning the key in the lock I went indoors. The hallway was not gloomy as it had been. The woodwork was painted white and the wallpaper was a very light grey. A side window had been put in and there were pretty lamps along the wall with a thick grey tufted carpet on the floor. The hall did not seem so narrow now or as long.

I walked through to the kitchen, which had a tiled floor and pine cupboards along the walls. The dividing wall of the back place had been taken down, enlarging the kitchen. At the far end there was a window that had been put in, looking out onto the garden. I walked through into the dining room. The walls were pink-washed and the carpet was a flecked cream. I walked back along the hall through to the front room, which like the other rooms was lighter, decorated in peach and white. There was a wood burner where the coal fire had been. The blue shiny tiles around the fireplace were still there.

The stairs had edge-to-edge grey carpeting on. I remembered sweeping the stairs and dusting the wood of them. My bedroom was now a bathroom. The three remaining bedrooms were painted in light, bright colours and had fitted pine wardrobes. There was a separate upstairs loo where there had been a cupboard and, as the blurb about the house said, there was central heating throughout.

I walked around the house again, taking time as I did so. The house as I remembered it wasn't there anymore but had been replaced by the individuality of other residents.

The yard outside was shingled. The small lawn was surrounded by landscaped borders beyond which was a brick garage and beyond that, where the strawberries had grown and the apple tree had been, was a high wooden fence and a new house. A shaft of sadness went through me as I remembered being a small child with strawberry juice running down my chin.

Returning to the house I left and locked the door. As I did so I heard a faint echo. I held my breath as all the ghosts of the past scampered away.

Chapter Thirteen

In 1984 after my mother died, I cleared her house and found a small, worn brown leather purse. Inside was a thin piece of paper folded into a small square. The paper had the date 1963 and the words: Nicholls Lance Corporal T W, 3rd May 1917 Age 39 – Household Battalion. Arras memorial, France. Bay 1. Arras was in capital letters and had been misspelt and corrected and the word France was underlined.

The paper, folded over into a small square, looked as if it had been read many times. My mother had never mentioned it to me, but now looking at it, it almost seemed liked a talisman. I felt that it had given my mother a connection with her father. I returned the paper to the purse and put it into a tin where I kept other pieces of family information. I did wonder who had written the words out for my mother and who had told her about the memorial in Bay 1.

***

I forgot about the paper until my friends Mary and Vic Stanbrook suggested that Gary and myself might like to go with them on a five-day trip to France. "We're going to the Normandy Area," Vic said. "I want to visit a war grave whilst I am there."

"My grandfather has a memorial there somewhere," I replied. "At Arras."

"We'll go there then," Vic said.

We went to France using the channel tunnel. From Calais, Vic drove to St Omer and then onto Arras. On our arrival at Arras we parked up and walked around until we found a place to stay. It was a modern hotel called Hotel Ibis in a quiet corner of the town overlooking a small square, which had the name Ipswich on a plaque. Gary and Vic went back to fetch the car whilst Mary and I had a quick look around at some of the bakery shops.

After breakfast the next day we had a look around Arras, walking around a market that was set out in the square. We went into the large cathedral and had a tour of a labyrinth of underground tunnels. During the war the French and English soldiers as well as other nationalities had hidden here. The Germans had no idea that the tunnels were there. Towards the end of the tour we were shown the tunnels that had been filled with pots of ferns and orchids. They had artificial light on them and were watered by the moisture in the tunnels.

We had coffee in the square before moving on to the Arras War Cemetery. I had never expected to see it.

At the memorial, with Vic's help and the help of an attendant, we had found the name we were looking for amongst the hundreds of others that were there. The attendant poured water on the engraved letters so the words showed up to enable me to take a photograph. I wondered where my grandfather had been killed. I looked around and thought of his bones and his name tag lying in a field somewhere in France. I was overcome with unexpected emotion at seeing the name of the man I had heard spoken of so often. I wrote in the visitors' book: To the memory of my Grandfather TW Nicholls, whose death affected so many.

As I walked back to the car I remembered my mother telling me that her last memory of her father had been when she was six. He'd hired a pony and trap and taken the family to the seaside for the day.

We left the cemetery and drove towards Les Andeley, stopping to eat our picnic before continuing towards our accommodation. I looked out of the window and wondered if my grandfather had seen these same fields. He must have written letters home during the time that he was in France in the August until the May, but I had found nothing relating to him when I cleared the house out.

Our last night was spent at Honfleur in a hotel, which overlooked a marina. The skies were grey and there was a light drizzle of rain and the place reminded me of Cornwall. In the evening we walked around the cobbled streets and I looked in the small shop windows. Mary had told me that unlike England, France still had many small specialist shops selling things such as tapestries, cottons or glassware. As we had walked back to the hotel I saw the bright window of a hat and accessory shop. The colours caught my eye and for no reason I took a picture. When I got home I put the picture into my photo album alongside the picture of me pointing to my grandfather's name at the Arras War Memorial.

On the shelf in my room I have a large copper disc with his name on. There is a man holding a laurel wreath above the name and the words around it say: He died for freedom and honour.

***

When I returned to England, I spoke to John Haygarth who lived in Bruisyard and who was the secretary to the Suffolk Western Front. John was writing a book about people from Framlingham who were killed in the First World War. When he died, the book was completed by a lady called Evelyn Epson. It was really due to John's efforts that I learned about the cemetery in Arras. He told me that the battle in which my grandfather died was called the Third Battle of the River Scarpe and it took place at Rouex, which is about 10 miles from Arras. The battle started at 4am and was a huge manoeuvre to try and take a nearby chemical factory. The battle took place on a high hill near the River Monchet. According to John, the soldiers never stood a chance. It was the third battle to try and take this area, which had started at Fampaux on Easter Sunday. The entire battalion was wiped out. There is now a local cemetery in the place where the battle was, so my grandfather's remains lay, although unmarked, in a cemetery.

Chapter Fourteen

I married John Clack on October 26, 1963. I was 19 years old. We had three children; Sarah Jane, born October 14, 1964, Selena Mary, born February 11, 1967 and John Benjamin (known as JB) born March 20, 1977. Sarah married Kim Knights on November 11, 1994 and they had three children, Laura Jane, born July 22, 1986, Chloe Marie, born December 14, 1988 and Daniel Jon, born January 18, 1990. Sarah and Kim were divorced some years later.

Selena married Richard Coles on July 2, 1994 and they had two sons, Adam Richard, born October 22, 1997 and Ryan John, born on February 1, 2000. John (JB) married Keeley Gladwell nee Brown, on June 5, 2004. My husband, John Clack, died in Norwich Hospital on February 5, 1989 and on December 24, 1999, I married Gary Bloom.

These are the facts, which relate nothing about the people, especially those of long ago. How I wished I had asked more questions. I hope that anyone reading this will ask questions before it is too late. As one gets older the past and the history of one's relatives and what makes them tick becomes more and more interesting.

***

Several years ago, I began sorting through piles of old photographs. I had been meaning to get them into some sort of order for years. I put them in envelopes with dates on.

"I hope you finish this before you die, Mum," my daughter Selena said. "Otherwise we won't know who all these people are."

Looking through the faded sepia photos I didn't know who some of the people were myself. I had come across many of them when sorting my mother's things after her death. I had found a lovely one of my mother that was taken when she was about 20. It was a big picture that I had not seen before and on the day of her funeral, I'd propped it up against a vase of flowers on the windowsill. When the rector, Father Lovejoy, who had taken the service came back for a cup of tea, he had looked at it and asked me who it was.

"My mother," I had replied, surprised that he had not recognised her. Looking again, he said, "Ah yes, of course. I can see the resemblance now."

Now, sifting through the photos, I studied the unfamiliar faces and sorted them into untidy piles. The 'don't know' and 'not sure' piles grew larger as I looked at faces of ladies in long black dresses who gazed back at me. There were small children too. There was Bill, and in one picture he stood with his two sisters. His outfit looked like a dress, the style of the day for young children. The two girls standing beside him were my mother and her sister, aged about two and three years old. They had long, waved hair. Their eyes looked bright and optimistic. I started a new pile with pictures of my mother at the seaside as a young woman.

I lifted another batch of photographs out of the large

oak chest. These were easier to put into order because the names were written on the back. There were pictures of three elegant ladies in long Edwardian dresses. Beside the names of the Crane sisters was written The Three Graces. These were pictures of my Grandmother and my great aunts. The next photograph out of the box was a larger one with Uncle Bert written on. This was my great uncle who my son John resembles. Uncle Bert had been a dentist in Northampton. Sitting back on my heels, I thought of the family. It starts as a small unit, then spreads and separates; relations becoming more distant, setting up their own groups, which in turn spread out becoming yet more distant again.

I'd bought a large blue covered album that had tissue paper between the leaves for the photos. I put a label on the front and printed the words: Family Album – Nicholls and Cranes, and then added: Mary Nicholls, in memory.

The first picture was of William Crane who was the grandfather of my grandmother. I had a family tree that was sent me so I knew he was born in the early 1800s. I looked at the picture. He had curly hair, a round face and side whiskers. There was a small pin pressed into the tie around his neck and a watch chain hanging on the front of his waistcoat.

On the next page I put in the pictures of William's son Thomas and his wife Emma whom he had married in 1877. In the picture they are sitting side by side. Emma looks younger than her husband. He has a heavy brown moustache and a good head of dark hair and like his father he has a watch chain around his waistcoat. Maybe the same one, I thought. He had lovely eyes set wide apart. He looked a kindly man but very serious. Emma was smiling. She wore a dark dress with a high collar with a brooch pinned on it. Thomas had died in 1922, but not before he had fathered seven children.

According to the family tree, two daughters, Kate and Alice, had died spinsters. William had died at the age of two; Harry, who had been a saddler, had married and had two children. Frederick had also married and had one child and Herbert had been a dentist and had had two sons, and then there was Ada, my grandmother.

On the next page I put in two separate pictures of Emma and Thomas and turning the page again, I headed it Yarmouth, August 1925. In the centre of the page I put in a large studio picture of Emma as an old lady. She wore a hat covered in ostrich feathers with one large one sticking up in the air. She still had the same enigmatic smile and the brooch on her high collar seemed to be the same one that she wore in earlier pictures. The small pictures that I put around the edges showed Emma at the seaside and in a wheelchair. In one of the pictures she has her hat off and it shows her mass of white hair. She is with her daughters, Kate and Alice.

My grandmother Ada Crane comes next in the album. There are some beautiful pictures of her and I enjoy putting these in the book. Her dark hair is piled up and, as is the fashion, she has on a dress with a high collar. I think she looks very wistful in these photos.

I find a picture of the three sisters, Alice, Kit and Ada – The Three Graces. They are posing in a studio, which is made to look like the seaside. All are wearing long skirts and blouses with high collars. Kit is sitting on a rock and Ada sits demurely in a deck chair. Alice stands behind, her arm resting on Kit's shoulder. To this page I add pictures of Bert the dentist and Harry, the saddler.

It is time for the Nicholls entry now and I add pictures of Tom Nicholls who married Ada in 1907. He looks very handsome and is sitting back to front on a chair with his arms resting on the back. He has a pipe in his hand and is wearing a suit and white shirt with a high collar and tie. On his head he has a very peculiar looking hat. It is checkered and looks like a raised cap without a peak. The next pictures are of Tom in uniform. I realise my grandmother was only married for 10 years and a widow for 47. There is one of Tom taken when he was 17, again in uniform. This was when he fought in South Africa in the Boer War.

There is one more of him and this time he is standing with his wife who is pregnant with their first child. Tom has a straw boater and a tight-fitting suit on and his arms are behind his back. Tom and Ada's first child Bill was born in 1909 and there are pictures of him in a white frilly dress, aged about one year. He is holding a teddy bear and there is a dog sitting under the chair. Beside him he has a small toy horse on wheels. Bill's birth is followed one year later by the arrival of Gladys (Dah) and then a year after that my mother Mary is born in 1911. The next three pages are filled with pictures of these children. I see my mother when she was aged two, again aged three, chubby faced, long haired and smiling. The girls wear white smocks and brown boots. Bill is dressed in a white jumper and short trousers.

I continue the album and come across a lovely one taken outside my mother's home. Seated in a wicker chair is Thomas Crane's sister, another Emma. On either side are Ada's two daughters, Mary and Gladys (Dah), both wearing straw hats with a large bow on and dresses with a low waist with bows tied around the dresses and they have on long white socks and white shoes. Behind Emma stands Bill wearing the uniform of Framlingham College, which includes a small cap, which is something boys would not be seen dead in now. The pages that follow are filled with pictures of my mother in her school days and later on when she was at the beach. In her school days she has long plaits and is taller than her contemporaries. In all of them she is laughing and the happiest ones are of her taken at Thorpeness in her 20s. She looks sun tanned and wears an attractive swimming costume, which is very modern in style for the era. She is with her brother Bill and her sister, Gladys (Dah) and friends. They appear to have had lovely times on the beach and in the sea. My Mum looks so happy lying on the beach or laughing with her sister, sitting beside her brother or just splashing about in the sea. My grandmother Ada is also in some of the pictures, wearing a dark dress and knitting, even on what seems to be the hottest of days.

There are studio pictures taken of my mother when she was 16, wearing a pretty dress and a row of pearls. These pictures show her lovely, thick, wavy hair. There are pictures of her in the local amateur dramatic group and also in the Framlingham Pageant in 1931. In some of the pictures there are the aunts, Kit and Alice, and in one Alice is wearing a swimming costume. I cannot connect the austere and heavily dressed woman I knew with this picture, nor could I imagine Auntie Alice ever swimming in the sea.

I continue the album. I put in more pictures of my mother taken on later days. She never recovered from the death of her brother or from the shame of the divorce, but maybe it all started with the death of her father. I put in pictures of Gladys. She married later in life but did not have a family. I never knew her as she appeared in the pictures, which was when she seemed really happy and when she and my mother seemed close.

There are two pages dedicated to my grandmother. There are coloured pictures of her in her beloved garden taken by the American serviceman, Bill Kloeblem, that she befriended during the Second World War. They had the luxury of colour films, which we didn't. There is one of her in the 1931 Framlingham Pageant and another of her beaming in her kitchen. The year is 1944 and she is taking the Christmas turkey out of the oven. She also played bowls and is seen in a picture wearing a suit and flat brown shoes at the Framlingham bowling club at the age of 52 but looking much older.

I find gorgeous pictures of Auntie Kit and Alice that should have gone into the album sooner. They were beautiful woman of the Edwardian era. Kit was the prettiest with large eyes and a beautifully shaped mouth and thick hair. Both the sisters were engaged at one time, but their fiancées were killed in the war. In later years Auntie Kit took to having the vapours, which was fainting or swooning and then having to have smelling salts administered.

There is one double page left in the book. I want to end with my mother. I put in a very early studio picture, full faced and smiling and then one taken in the garden with her Airedale dog, Jean. She is kneeling down with the dog and her short-waved hair is clipped back. Underneath this picture I write: I wanted to end the book with a picture of my mother, Mary Margaret Nicholls, later Webber, and then Stainbank. Getting these photographs together in one collection is a dedication to her and the Crane/Nicholls family. Her life did not go according to plan and the early happy years are good to see because her later years bought so much sadness and ill health to her. My Mum was a kind lady with little thought for herself. This is her book from her loving daughter.

***

I picked up another photo album and a black and white picture fell from the pages. It was of me, aged 17, slim, bikini clad, laughing. *Was I ever as thin as that?* I wondered. I noticed that the photo was frayed around the edges and remembered that my husband John used to carry it about in his wallet. It had been taken when I had been sitting beside a large open-air swimming pool in Northampton one very hot summer. I had been with my friend Carol. We were both 17. I had posed by the steps of the pool, feeling very self-conscious as I did so. Hmm, I look quite glamorous, I thought. My face looked a bit fuzzy but I was laughing in it. Now it was just another loose picture to put somewhere. Maybe just in a chronological order would do, with as many names as I could remember written down.

I heard the front door bang. "Hi Nan," a voice said. It was my 10-year-old grandson Dan coming to visit me on his way home from school. I hadn't realized the time.

"I'm through here sorting out old photos," I shouted. "There's a drink and biscuits on the side for you."

He came through into the room. "Can I go on the computer, Nan?" he asked.

"Of course," I said. "But come here first." I picked up the

photo of myself. "Do you know who this is Dan?" I asked.

"Yeah, it's you," he said.

I was surprised. "How did you know that?" I asked.

"By the face of course," he replied. He grinned. "How else?"

And he went upstairs to turn on the computer.

***

I had emptied the walnut-veneered box of its contents. I hadn't done it methodically, just tipped everything out onto the bed. A pile of documents lay scattered on the creased bedspread. Among them lay a paper clip, a cufflink, a hair grip, three odd earrings and a medal with a faded blue and orange ribbon on it. I picked up the document nearest to me. It was my grandmother's birth certificate, and folded inside was her marriage certificate.

My grandmother had been dead for over 40 years. I hadn't a clue what to do with all this stuff. What I needed was a system. I would throw out anything that wasn't of interest, I decided. But then again? Maybe in years to come these faded documents would be of interest to someone searching through their family tree. And that was another question – how did people know if they were related? People strayed and a baby's father is not always the one that is named on the birth certificate.

I picked up a small, faded piece of card with a scalloped silver edge. The words read: St Sepulchre's Church, May 20th 1907, with compliments, Mr. and Mrs. TW Nicholls. Underneath was the address where my grandmother had spent much of her married life. Printed next to that was the name Ada Crane, her maiden name with a silver arrow through it. It was a marriage announcement. I put it to one side. I couldn't throw that away. It was nearly one hundred years old.

The next item was a faded cutting from a newspaper. There was no date, but the items listed for sale on one side of the paper showed it to be about 70 years old. Turning it over, I read the rules printed on the other side under the heading:

Something of Interest to Women – Rules for Health.

Don't worry.

Don't hurry. Too swift arrives as tardy as slow.

Be regular. Be sympathetic. Order is Heaven's first law.

Don't over eat. Don't starve. Let your moderation be known to all men.

Sleep and rest abundantly. Sleep is nature's great restorer.

Court fresh air day and night. Learn how to breathe. The breath of life is in the air.

Leave a margin of nervous energy for tomorrow.

Don't spend faster than you make.

Be cheerful. A light heart lives long.

Work diligently, but don't be worked to death.

Avoid passion and excitement. A moment's anger may cause life-long misery. Seek peace and ensue it.

Think only beautiful thoughts. As a man thinketh in his heart, so is he. Forget yourself in living for others.

Look for the good in everybody and everything.

I thought that these sensible rules of life don't change much. I feel that one needs passion and excitement in life, but since I like the sentiments in the rules, I laid them on the pile of things to keep.

I picked up birth certificates and death certificates, records of people long gone. There was a small scrap of paper with the name of my grandfather and the details of his memorial in France. It was his name on the medal that had the blue and gold ribbon attached. Everything I picked up was something that may one day interest someone.

I looked in the empty box. A small piece of faded newspaper was stuck under a join in the wood: Nicholls – On September 4th, 1965 at home, Ada, widow of Thomas William Nicholls and beloved mother of Gladys, Mary and the late William and loving grandmother of …

And so it went on with details of the funeral service at Framlingham church at 11.15am on Wednesday, September 8, 1965.

I thought of my grandmother who had given my mother and I a home after my parents' divorce. I remembered that I was the only child with divorced parents in the whole school. Nowadays I would probably be part of the majority.

I threw away the paper clips, the odd earrings, the cufflink and the hair grip, but I returned my grandfather's medal and all the other documents to the box.

***

The colours are brown, sepia I suppose you would call it. It is, by my assumption, a sad photo because no one is smiling and the expressions on the faces are, I would say, without joy. It is a photograph of my grandmother, Ada Nicholls with her three children. My grandmother is looking above the heads of the children into the middle distance. I wonder what she was thinking.

At the bottom of the photograph is the name of the man who took it. It is CF Dowsing of Framlingham. He would have lived in Double Street, which at that time was called Bow Street because of the shape of it. It would have been a busy street then, with a bakers' shop and a pub and a tailors and even a library at one time. Now it is just a street of houses.

In the photograph my grandmother's arms hold two of her children, whilst the third, Gladys, sits on the chair. It would have been taken just after the end of the Great War. Maybe it is my grandfather that my grandmother is thinking about.

Chapter Fifteen

The Presence of my Grandfather

November 2012

In the corner of my garden is an old hawthorn tree. Its scabby
trunk leans over to one side. The branches are lichen covered
and most are dead. In the spring time, when I first moved to
the house, the tree would be covered with a mass of white may
blossom and then in autumn, bright red berries but not now. It is
dying, worn out from old age.

When the blossom fell off I could see the small green hard
berries that even in the spring were there, a sign of winter. And
then when all the leaves were off the branches I would look again
and see buds forming ready for the spring. The berries were eaten
by the birds, usually a blackbird who in the dark days of winter,
silhouetted against the sky, would perch on a high branch and
sing out his clear notes.

The tree was there when my grandfather was alive, before he was
killed in the Great War. He lived in a house at the top of the road,
not far from where I live now. I feel sure that he would have looked
out of his window and seen the blossom of that tree or maybe
noticed it as he walked down the road and passed my house.

I thought about him today. Maybe it is all the stuff about the war that is on at the moment. I thought about how my grandmother and mother never went to Remembrance Day services, although they had lost the two people they had loved more than anyone else in the world. They both said that they didn't need a service to remember them by as they thought about them every day in their own way.

To return to my grandfather, I was looking at the tree and thinking of him. In his photos, he wears clothes that make him look older and different from the young men of today. He wasn't much older than my son when he went to war and I imagined what JB would have felt like going off to fight and leaving his wife and young sons behind. What I have written below, somehow it seems to put it all into perspective about the man I knew only by name and old black and white pictures.

Later that day I went to the birthday party of my middle great grandchild, three-year-old Mia. There was a room full of young children with their parents. My eldest granddaughter Laura was there with her daughter, six-week-old Lydia. Mia's grandmother, my daughter Sarah, was there too. I perched on the settee on the perimeter of the activity, feeling overwhelmed by youth and family.

My granddaughter Chloe, Mia's Mum, bought in a Tesco birthday cake. It was iced in bright pink and had three candles and a plastic Peppa Pig on the top. We sang Happy Birthday and Mia's delighted face glowed in the brightness of the candles. She blew them out and wanted to do it all over again, which she did with the help of her sister, Rhianna. After a couple of hours I felt it was time for me to leave and standing up I stepped over wrapping paper and plastic toys and balloons to kiss Mia and

other family members goodbye and I returned home. I glance at
the hawthorn tree as I enter the garden. I notice that the last few
leaves have fallen from the dying branch. I think again of my
grandfather who never had the chance to meet his descendants.

***

The Wedding

September 8, 2011

My granddaughter, Chloe, is getting married to Liam at the
local church. They have two children, Rhianna and Mia. There
are 40 guests inside the church. The colour theme is purple and
both myself and my daughter Sarah are wearing an outfit to tie
in with the theme.

The organist starts to play and the congregation stands. I
turn to watch Chloe enter the church. There are three adult
bridesmaids wearing purple dresses and carrying a small posy
of white rose buds. Rihanna and Mia are the flower girls. They
wear white dresses with sparkles of stars on and carry a small
basket of flowers. They smile and look around as they walk
down the aisle. Chloe's brother Dan is giving her away and
Chloe, as all brides should, looks radiant.

I sit down remembering my own marriage in the same church
in 1963. I also remember other occasions that have taken place
in this church. There were the marriages of my two younger
children, Selena and John (JB), five christenings and three
funerals that were my grandmother's, my mother's and John, my
husband's in 1989.

The Reverend Graham Owen looks around, smiles and begins the service: "God is love and those who live in love live in God." Liam beams at Chloe and takes her hand. Mia wanders off around the church. Laura who is the bride's sister and the chief bridesmaid goes after her. I find it hard to keep the image of my marriage from my mind. It seems no time at all since I walked up the same aisle towards John, who turned around to watch me.

Sunlight pierces the clear glass of the east window and the long beam slants down onto Chloe and Liam as they make their vows. Chloe sobs her way through them. Neither the best man nor Dan has a handkerchief so a member of the congregation hands her one.

The congregation rises to sing a hymn. Then there are prayers and another hymn and the newlyweds sign the register. When this is done they walk back down the aisle. The church bells ring out and they go out into the sunshine followed by their guests who stand around chatting whilst endless photographs are taken.

I stand beside the war memorial. The black writing has gone and there is just an indentation of the names in the stone. I read the name of my grandfather, Chloe's two times great grandfather, TW Nicholls, the man who went to war and didn't return.

***

What I Learnt

Shopping in the Co-op, Gary picked up a bag of cooked beetroot. I had forgotten that Gary liked it. "I can cook some fresh," I said. "I wonder how many young people know how to cook beetroot or if they would even bother."

Before you start, beetroot has to be scrubbed clean. Cut off the leaves – not too near to the beet or it will bleed. Put into boiling water and cook until soft, about half an hour or so. I never time it. Take it out of the water. When cool, peel off the skin. Slice it or leave whole and cover with vinegar. It does make your urine pink, nothing to worry about, it is just the beetroot.

Thinking about this got me wondering about other things I learned to do when I was a child, by watching or later by being taught.

I am proud of the fact I can skin a rabbit, pluck a chicken or a pheasant and draw a bird ready for the table. I can light a paraffin lamp, trim a wick of the same. I can chop kindling, collect sticks for a fire, chop up wood for logs and get a fire going by holding large sheets of newspaper against the surrounding tiles. I can make a wool rug, crochet a jumper, darn socks, replace a broken zip and sew on buttons. I know that to keep runner beans fresh, you wrap them in newspaper and to keep cut flowers fresh until you can put them in water, wrap wet newspaper around the bottom of the stalks. Slugs are kept away from plants by putting a trail of salt around the plant. Salt dries up their slime. I know that to store apples you must lay them so they do not touch each other, as a rotten apple will turn the others rotten.

***

It is 2014, and in seven days' time it will be Christmas. At the local church, St Michael's, there is a Christmas tree event. This is something that happens each year, despite the fact that Christmas trees are pagan symbols. But this festival has caught the imagination of churches throughout the UK.

I am taking my great-granddaughter, two-year-old Lydia, so that she can see the sparkling trees, lit with coloured lights. As we are about to enter the church I notice the winter sun reflecting on a piece of black flint in the stone work, beside which trails a rose bush. It has one pink bloom on it. The petals are faded, tinged brown at the edges. Lydia runs on ahead, her footsteps echoing around the church and up into the high arched roof. A happy child always full of laughter, Lydia giggles at this.

There are 15 trees in the church, donated by local businesses and organisations. Not interested in the trees, Lydia finds the children's corner. She rearranges the cushions on the floor and then picks up a drum, which she bangs on with her small fists.

Just down the steps from that corner there are three British Legion Standards propped against the wall where there is a photographic and written memorial to the fallen of the Great War. In the top right corner is a picture of a good-looking man called Thomas William Nicholls. The records say that he was killed in 1915 at the age of 39 in Arras, France.

I take Lydia's hand. She hops and skips, from one foot to the other, her dark, brown hair, tied in bunches, flicks against her neck. I stand looking at the picture of the man Tom Nicholls, who is my grandfather and who died 29 years before I was born. In the photograph he appears to be looking down at Lydia, his three times great-granddaughter.

Lydia, impatient to be off, moves away and runs to the door of the church. Outside now, the sun has gone in. The few pink petals of the singular rose have fallen to the ground. Lydia bends to pick them up, but a sharp breeze blows them along the gravel pathway. She chases after them. I follow her, glancing from habit at the war memorial. Lydia chases around it, out of sight for moment before reappearing, with one pink petal in her hand.

***

I showed the pictures of my grandmother with her sisters, and one of her with her three children, to my great granddaughter, Rhianna. I counted the generations backwards. "This is your great, great, great, grandmother!" I told her.

"They look like ghosts," Rhianna's mother Chloe said.

I looked at them. They were ghosts, people from another age who continue to haunt me.

More recently, Chloe, now 30, said to me as we walked round an old part of Fram cemetery, "These people may be dead, but they live on with us chatting about the names on the headstones."

***

My memories tumble over many decades. I straddle generations. I was born in 1944. My Edwardian grandmother was born in 1884 and my mother was born in the 1920s. My children, grandchildren and great grandchildren were born in the 20th and 21st centuries. Six generations – amazing. The nature of life is change and that is how it should be.

Nannies's descendants. Me, Jane, seated with two of my children, my grandchildren and great-grandchildren in December, 2017.